"Winds of social and spiritual turmoil are ___
Planted, Pastor Robby Gallaty provides bibli ___
stabilize any follower of Jesus. I highly rec ___

Steve Gaines, Ph.D., Senior Pastor
Bellevue Baptist Church

"So grateful for how Robby uses his giftedness to bring clarity to biblical teaching while also helping to make disciples that make disciples. I am being helped as a pastor to better lead His people thanks to *Firmly Planted.*

Johnny Hunt, Senior Pastor
First Baptist Woodstock

"*Firmly Planted* is the second in a Trilogy dedicated to discipleship-making. It addresses with clarity and biblical faithfulness crucial issues to growing up in Christlikeness. I like this series and I am delighted to commend it's use in churches committed to multiply Christ followers."

Daniel L. Akin, President
Southeastern Baptist Theological Seminary

"The evangelical church is facing its greatest crisis of my lifetime. It is an identity crisis in which the people inside our churches are looking more and more like the people outside our churches. We must do a better job of making disciples who look and live like Jesus. If you want a church to be more fruitful in evangelism, give more attention to discipleship. Pastor Robby Gallaty has produced and excellent tool to help you do so. Get it read it, and thank me later!"

Dr. Charles S. Kelley, President
New Orleans Baptist Theological Seminary

"*Firmly Planted* is so timely. Attacks are relentlessly unleashing from the enemy and the church must equip themselves for the war. This book provides those tools. You'll love this book because it is inspired from real life. I have witnessed Robby go to battle preaching the Gospel at our church in New Orleans, building an army of discipleship groups in his church in Chattanooga, and now through writing this powerful book. Thank you Robby for equipping the saints in this crucial time. Who Dat!"

Rob Wilton, Lead Pastor
Vintage Church

"In many parts of the world, Christianity is suffering from stunted growth. While people might have some religious knowledge, they have failed to move forward in the spiritual growth God intends for all His children. I'm thankful for the voice of Robby Gallaty who is waving the banner of growth and discipleship. *Firmly Planted* is a biblically faithful, grace saturated, and Christ exalting charge to actively fight against the temptation toward stagnation and instead embrace the work of God in a person›s life that propels us forward in spiritual growth."

Michael Kelley, Director of Groups Ministry
LifeWay Christian Resources

"Robby Gallaty has provided in *Firmly Planted* a great tool to help new believers and growing Christians succeed in going to the next level in their relationship with Christ. *Firmly Planted* is a great resources for spiritual formation."

Steve Stroope, Lead Pastor, Lake Pointe Church
Author, *Tribal Church*

"If someone asks you: 'How do you know for sure you're saved and that you will live with God for eternity?' Would you be able to defend that biblical teaching? Many people in our churches will testify to being saved by the gospel of Jesus Christ, but when asked to defend how they know they're saved and explain it with confidence, many just can't — but they should. The average Christian just isn't equipped in this regard. In his new book, Pastor Robby not only presents the salvation message, but shares the full-depth of what it actually means and how to explain salvation and defend it to others. He also helps readers understand the enemies in the enormous spiritual battle that surrounds us. As a Bible-equipping ministry, AiG is happy to come alongside Robby and see more Christians equipped in biblical truths, such as our precious salvation in Christ."

Ken Ham, President/CEO Answers in Genesis
Creation Museum

"Robby Gallaty has written a very practical, helpful, and compelling book that will become a giant in the marketplace. *Firmly Planted* can be a catalyst in your walk with Christ and for discipling others in their walk with God. Every Christ-follower and church needs, *Firmly Planted.*"

Ronnie Floyd, President of the Southern Baptist Convention
Senior Pastor, Cross Church

"No single person has influenced me in the area of discipleship more than Robby Gallaty. His first book, *Growing Up*, is a necessary roadmap toward making disciples. Now, in *Firmly Planted*, Robby points us to the desired destination of every Christ follower. The former equips us with strategy; the latter encourages us with stability. By anticipating the biblical thinking required to thrive as a disciple in various life situations, this new addition to the Growing Up Series highlights the natural progression of maturity, helping readers undergird their disciplines for the Lord with deeper devotion to the Lord. I cannot wait to share it in my D-groups!"

Adam Dooley, Senior Pastor
Sunnyvale First Baptist

"Too often I judge my standing with God on how I feel. I don't think I'm alone in that. Robby Gallaty takes the Word of God to drive us away from our morbid introspection, and fixes our gaze where ought to be: on Christ and his gospel. Along the way he shows us how to fight the devil, not with our own power but with Empty Tomb glory. Read this book, be encouraged, and then pass it on to a fellow pilgrim."

Russell D. Moore, President
Southern Baptist Ethics & Religious Liberty Commission

"Robby Gallaty, in this realistically practical book, with Bible in hand, leads a disciple in the way of victorious living in Christ. Right on Target!"

Robert E. Coleman
Author of *The Master Plan of Evangelism*

"Spiritual immaturity has ravaged individual Christians like a plague since the inception of the church nearly 2,000 years ago. Indeed, much of the New Testament was written to correct false ideas about the gospel, false ideas about Christ, false ideas about Christian living, and to challenge Christians to overcome the spiritual inertia of a weak faith. In *Firmly Planted*, Dr. Robby Gallaty has provided the church with a wonderful synthesis of New Testament teaching on these issues. His work provides an outstanding introduction to the basics of the Christian faith in a manner that will equip individual Christians and small groups alike to grow into Christian maturity and live lives that bring great glory to Jesus Christ. I highly recommend *Firmly Planted* for use in your church."

Thom S. Rainer, President and CEO
LifeWay Christian Resources

Firmly Planted

How To Cultivate a Faith Rooted in Christ

Robby Gallaty

PUBLISHING GROUP

Nashville, Tennessee

Book 1

Growing Up
Psalm 1:1-2

Blessed is the man who walks not in the counsel of the wicked,
nor stands in the way of sinners, nor sits in the seat of scoffers;
but his delight is in the law of the Lord, and on his law
he meditates day and night.

Book 2

Firmly Planted
Psalm 1:3

He is like a tree planted by streams of water...

Book 3

Bearing Fruit
Psalm 1:3b

...that yields its fruit in its season, and its leaf does not wither.
In all that he does, he prospers.

To

Tim LaFleur

I will never forget those late nights we spent unpacking doctrines of the faith during the summer of 2003 in Glorieta, NM. You have been a friend, ministry partner, and father in the faith

Thank you for investing your life into mine.

Contents

Foreword

Church leaders often forget that new congregation members need to be equipped. There is a lot of focus on gathering new people and assimilating them into relational units. These units are typically small groups or affinity-based groups that don't do any serious training. This can often lead to people who are "assimilated" relationally but remain untrained. Can you imagine a church populated with 50-75% of their members untrained and unprepared to be and do what the pastor calls them to be and do every week? This is not only frustrating, it is tragic because Christ calls all members to be the salt of the earth and the light of the world. It is like sending soldiers to fight in a war without the knowledge, skill or equipment to fight.

I am so glad that Dr. Robby Gallaty has written this crucial book that guides readers into the training that is needed. Every important piece of equipment is explained in detail; it begins with who we are and what we have, and moves on to overcoming the challenges of spiritual warfare. This is the basic training that is at the heart of discipleship. It is time for many churches to circle back and train their soldiers. If you are a pastor or teacher and wonder why your people are not moving forward with confidence in their faith, then open this book and learn. If you are one of the multitude of the untrained, open these pages and drink it in. You will sense God's power growing in you.

Bill Hull
Author of *Jesus Christ Disciple Maker,*
The Disciple Making Pastor,
The Disciple Making Church, and *Conversion Discipleship.*

Introduction

Growing up, I loved the game of basketball. Like most boys raised in the 90's, I wished I could be "like Mike." Though Michael Jordan and I are the same height, we played different positions: he was a guard; I was a center. In high school, I was taller than most of my friends—in fact, it wasn't until college that I was dwarfed by some of my teammates.

As a center, the majority of my duties revolved around the area near the goal. As the guard dribbled the ball down the court, I would run toward the lower corner of the paint, post up, and raise my hand to signal for the ball. The guard would then recognize I was in position to make a move on my opponent who was blocked by my back and a wide-leg stance.

Any good center knows that a strong base is a requirement for success. Without it, he'd be knocked down, pushed over, or bullied around. I spent many hours in the gym with knees bent, head up, and thighs burning as I held that position to strengthen my lower body for battle on game day. Just as a good foundation is necessary for any center in basketball, so also is it an essential component for a believer who desires to mature in the Christian life.

Spiritual immaturity is a plague that has infected many believers. Even the early church was not immune to the debilitating results of a shallow faith. Paul expressed his frustration with the lack of maturity among early believers in his letter to the Corinthian church: "I gave you milk to drink, not solid food, because you were not yet ready for it. In fact, you are still not ready, because you are still fleshly. For since there is envy and strife among you, are you not fleshly and living like unbelievers?" (1 Corinthians 3:2-3). He likens them to babies.

Let's get something straight about babies: they are cute. The way they coo and cuddle make them adorable. Kandi, my wife, often tells our young boys who are six and four, "Mommy wishes she could freeze you at this age forever!" We smile at their innocence, inquisitiveness, and dependence on us to help them understand this undiscovered world in which they live. However, you would admit that a 45-year old baby is appalling, not something to treasure.

Sadly, our churches are populated today with un-discipled believers who have attended church for many years but have never matured spiritually. No one took the time to walk with them through life's journey. A wealth of untapped resources occupies church pews every Sunday morning. Men and women who have the ability to reach the world with the gospel stream through our front doors, but they are unaware of their capability. Before we can mobilize this army of believers to go with the gospel, we must establish a firm foundation with the Word.

The Word Does the Work

From Genesis to Revelation, God established His purposes in His Word. In Genesis 1, the text repeats, "God *said*, 'Let there be light'"; "God *said*, 'Let there be an expanse between the waters'"; and "God *said*, 'Let the water under the sky be gathered into one place'" (Genesis 1:3, 6, 9; emphasis added). Repeatedly throughout the Old Testament, we witness the word of God coming to men and women, commanding and empowering them to do amazing things. The word of God came to Abraham in Genesis 12. It's impossible to overemphasize just how obedient Abraham was to leave his surroundings and travel to an unknown destination at the mere word from God. He obeyed a voice from heaven and it was "credited to his account as righteousness" (Genesis 15:6).

Moses heard the same voice calling out to him from the burning bush to approach Pharaoh, the "ruler of the land" at that time, with a request to relinquish God's people. Again, the word of God broke through the thunder and lightning on Mount Sinai in Exodus 20 with the commandments for the people to follow. With Moses' passing, God instructed Joshua, "Above all, be strong and very courageous to carefully observe the whole instruction my servant Moses commanded you. Do not turn from it to the right or the left, so that you will have success wherever you go" (Joshua 1:7).[1]

The prophet's job in the Old Testament was to recite the words of God to the people with perfect clarity and lucidity. Isaiah begins his book with these words: "Listen, heavens, and pay attention, earth, for the Lord has spoken" (Isaiah 1:2). In Chapter 55, God promises, "My word that comes from My mouth will not return to Me empty, but it will accomplish what I please and will prosper in what I send it to do" (Isaiah 55:11). Sixty times in the book of Ezekiel we find the phrase, "The word of the Lord came to me." The same phrase is used by the prophets Hosea, Joel, Amos, Micah, Zephaniah, Haggai, and Zechariah.

John the Baptist broke nearly 400 years of silence when he came as a "voice crying out in the wilderness" (Mark 1:3), preaching the word of God. In his gospel, John the Apostle clarifies Jesus' identity by stating, "In the beginning was the Word, and the Word was with God, and the Word was God. He was with God in the beginning. All things were created through Him, and apart from Him not one thing was created that has been created…. The Word became flesh and took up residence among us" (John 1:1-3, 14).

Paul instructs the Romans that "faith comes from what is heard, and what is heard comes through the message about Christ" (Romans 10:17) — from hearing the Word. In his final letter to Timothy, Paul emphasizes the importance of studying the Word: "Be diligent to present yourself approved to God, a worker who doesn't need to be ashamed, correctly teaching the word of truth" (2 Timothy 2:15). Likewise, the Apostle Peter states, "Since you have been born again — not of perishable seed but of imperishable — through the living and enduring word of God, for all flesh is like grass, and all its glory like a flower of the grass. The grass withers, and the flower falls, but the word of the

Lord endures forever" (1 Peter 1:23). Jesus' half-brother James, an unbeliever during Jesus' earthly ministry, penned these words years after Jesus' death: "Of his own will he brought us forth by the word of truth, that we should be a kind of first fruits of his creatures" (James 1:18, ESV).[2]

The author of Hebrews continuously cites the importance of the Word as well. Right out of the gate, he explains the source of all things saying, "The Son is the radiance of God's glory and the exact expression of His nature, sustaining all things by His powerful word" (Hebrews 1:3). Hebrews 4:12 explains the convicting nature of God's Word: "For the word of God is living and effective and sharper than any double-edged sword, penetrating as far as the separation of soul and spirit, joints and marrow. It is able to judge the ideas and thoughts of the heart." It's no wonder the Mishnah, a collection of the Jewish oral traditions, encourages followers of God to "Pore over it [the Scripture] again and again, for everything is contained in it; look into it, grow old and gray over it, and do not depart from it, for there is no better pursuit for you than this."[3]

It is Scripture's position that if change is going to happen, *we must get into the Word until the Word gets into us!*

Growing Up Series

Firmly Planted is the second of a three-book discipleship series. *Growing Up: How to Be a Disciple Who Makes Disciples*, the first book of the series, was released in November 2013. In *Growing Up*, I outlined the initial practices every believer should possess in making disciples who make disciples. *Growing Up* is divided into three basic sections. The first three chapters build a case for the necessity of making disciples. Chapter 4 deals with training yourself to become godly. The remaining six chapters, if incorporated into your life, will aid in developing a C.L.O.S.E.R. walk with Christ:

- *Communicate* with God through prayer
- *Learn* to understand and apply God's Word to your life

- *Obey* God's commands
- *Store* God's Word in your heart
- *Evangelize* (share Christ with others)
- *Renew* yourself spiritually every day

The C.L.O.S.E.R. acronym can be incorporated into any context, with any age group and maturity level. Book three of the series, *Bearing Fruit*, will be released in 2016.

Can I Be Firmly Planted?

Firmly Planted is saturated with theological insights, personal experiences, and practical applications to establish you as a stable, secure believer. Based on the conviction that a change of mind leads to a change of actions, the overall structure of the book is meant to ensure that readers are **well-equipped to enter and thrive amidst any situation life deals them.**

The first chapter establishes the nature of salvation: how God is the source of salvation and how Jesus is the cornerstone of salvation. Chapter 2 builds upon that truth, showing how one's assurance of salvation rests upon the promises of God's Word, the witness of God's Spirit, and the evidence of a changed life. Next, we discuss how the evidence of a changed life is a direct reflection of one's new identity in Christ (Chapter 3). Related to this important truth, we learn that not only are believers to be identified with Christ, but they are actually *united* with Christ to the degree that they both *recognize* and *reckon* their new relationship to Christ (Chapter 4).

Then, we discuss the war that rages between the believer and three spiritual enemies — the flesh (Chapter 5), the world (Chapter 6), and Satan (Chapter 7). With regard to the flesh, we examine how the flesh restrains one's response to God's work and reveals a heart alienated from God. With regard to the world, we dive into Paul's warning against the wickedness and worthlessness of worldliness. With regard to Satan, we provide a biblical profile of our nemesis as well as a glimpse of the God-empowered arms necessary to defeat him.

With the flesh, the world, and Satan standing as pervasive threats to the believer, we consider in Chapter 8 the source and sequence of temptation and outline what it takes to overcome it. The final two chapters offer a prescriptive battle plan for believers in the midst of spiritual warfare. The most effective way believers can become actively engaged in this plan is by equipping themselves with the proper attire for battle: the armor of God (Chapter 9), and prayer (Chapter 10). Prayer, we will argue, is perhaps the most powerful instrument a believer can take into battle.

Ideally, the material in the book should be discussed within a D-group: a gender-exclusive, closed group of three to six people who meet weekly. (For more information see Chapter 3 of *Growing Up*.) You can gather at someone's home, a restaurant, a break room at work, or at church for personal accountability, mutual edification, and spiritual enrichment.

As you study and grow, remember that you are not merely learning for your own benefit, but also for the benefit of others. Guiding others in their walk with Christ is a joy many overlook. The foremost way to make disciples is to become a disciple, and the only way to teach others effectively is to continue as a lifelong learner.

The topics in this book may be difficult to comprehend with only a cursory reading of each chapter. Much like a theological workbook for biblical training, each section should be walked through slowly. The material should be meditated upon and applied to your life.

Let's begin cultivating a firmly planted faith.

Chapter 1

Saved, Sure, and Secure:

Assurance of Salvation

Joe was one of the godliest men I knew. He served as the associate pastor of a church, headmaster of a Christian school, and leader of a Tuesday night Bible study I attended. His favorite topic was "losing your salvation." Every time he emphasized it, people got saved — some for the second, third, or fourth time. While his teaching on the subject was powerful to me as a new believer, I questioned if it was biblical.

As a direct result of Joe's teaching, I began researching what the Bible says about salvation. Clearly understanding that salvation is "by grace through faith" (Ephesians 2:8) and that we can do nothing to earn it, I came to a logical, firm conclusion: since we can do nothing good enough to achieve our salvation, we can do nothing bad enough to lose it.

Armed with the conviction of what Scripture clearly teaches, I decided to ask Joe about his position. "Brother Joe," I began, "you obviously believe that we can lose our salvation if we sin."

Confidently, he replied, "Yes, I do."

"What, then," I continued, "is your understanding of Ephesians 2:8-9 that states a believer is saved by grace and not works?"

The next ten minutes were like a Wild West shootout, with

Bible verses flying like bullets. I would shoot a verse at Joe, and he would fire back at me with another. The others in the group sat speechless as I, a young believer, questioned the seasoned leader of our Bible study. The gunfight finally ended when I said:

"Brother Joe, you are a godly man. All of your life, you have been faithful to the Lord, your wife, and your church. You have led a Christian school with integrity. Suppose that tonight, because you and I have had this dispute, you go away from this meeting with hatred in your heart toward me, which is a sin. As you are walking to your car, a truck strikes you, killing you instantly. Where are you going to spend eternity: heaven or hell?"

Without even pausing to consider the question, Joe looked me in the eye and said, "If I didn't repent before being hit by that truck, I would go to hell."

I was stunned. Speechless. Confused. Saddened by the error that robbed Joe of the joy of God's grace, I humbly replied, "The Bible doesn't teach that. I cannot agree with you."

It was my last Bible study with Brother Joe.

What puzzled me was that Joe was a staunch critic of the teaching that we are saved by our works. He regularly taught that we are saved by grace, apart from works. Yet, at the same time, he declared that sinful works can rob us of our salvation.

The fact is, you can't have it both ways: our works are either a part of salvation, or they are not. A salvation that is kept according to works is a salvation that is earned by works, which is not a biblical salvation. A salvation that is received by grace is entirely of grace, regardless of works. Period.

The equation for salvation is not:

Jesus + works = salvation

Nor is it:

Jesus + baptism,
Jesus + church membership,
Jesus + confession to a clergyman, or
Jesus + allegiance to the proper denomination = salvation.

Inspired by the Holy Spirit, Paul wrote, "For you are saved by grace through faith, and this is not from yourselves; it is God's gift — not from works, so that no one can boast" (Ephesians 2:8-9). Therefore, based on the simple teaching of Scripture, the equation for salvation is:

Jesus + nothing else = salvation.

You do not work for your salvation. You work from your salvation. When you surrendered your life to Christ, *you put as much faith as you had in as much of Jesus as you knew.* Therefore, since salvation is wholly by grace, you are secure in Christ through faith in Him. Understanding this essential truth is one of the basics of the Christian life and grasping this principle is important for several reasons.

First, failing to understand that salvation is wholly by grace potentially robs sincere believers of the joy of knowing they are kept by the power of God (1 Peter 1:5). The idea that eternal salvation can be lost is one that is conceived in the minds of men who do not fully understand the far-reaching effects of Christ's death and the power of grace. Your relationship with Christ is not based on your individual performance, but on Christ's finished work on the cross. Sadly, some teach that salvation is kept through human works in order to strike a "spirit of fear" (2 Timothy 1:7) in their church members, an oppressive teaching that will force them to faithfulness. Such teaching, while not changing the truth about salvation, threatens to replace the believer's joy with a spirit of coercion or obligation.

Second, if we are convinced that every sin we commit causes us to lose our salvation, our service to God will be hindered by a mentality of self-preservation. That is, if we are constantly consumed with our own spiritual standing before God, our attention will be diverted from God's glory and His kingdom. You will never be a firmly-planted believer until you understand what the Bible declares about the permanence of salvation. What I hope to accomplish in this book is to share with you a prescriptive way to know that your Christian faith is properly, scripturally grounded so that its roots run deep and may receive proper nourishment to bear excellent fruit.

What then *does* Scripture teach about the security of the believer? How can we know with all assurance that we have eternal life? To answer these questions, one must first understand the nature of salvation. In the rest of this chapter, we will unpack the biblical foundations of salvation upon which we can build a firm basis for the security of the believer.

Question to Consider

How does lacking assurance of salvation
rob a believer of joy in Christ and
prevent them from growing?

The Source of Salvation: God

As one of Jesus' closest followers, John knew the Lord well. In fact, Scripture suggests that John was closer to Jesus than any of His other disciples. Combating the heresy of his day, John composed a specific letter, 1 John, for the purpose of assuring genuine Christians of their salvation. After stating his case for the security of the believer, John summarizes his presentation with a simple, powerful statement:

And this is the testimony: God has given us eternal life, and this life
is in His Son (1 John 5:11).

In this verse, John reveals that God is the source of our salvation. Salvation comes from God. When we turn to Christ in faith and repent of our sins, God makes us eternally alive together with Christ (Ephesians 2:5). Notice that the verb "gave" is in the past tense, teaching us that eternal life is not something we have to wait for until we die. The moment you genuinely turned from sin and to Christ, God granted you entrance — once and for all — into His kingdom.

But what does John mean by "eternal life"? How can something that most Christians believe is granted in the future be given in the past? According to John, "eternal life" exists wholly and solely "in" Jesus Christ. At the beginning of his first letter, John authoritatively writes: "That life was revealed, and we have seen it and we testify and declare to you the eternal life that was with the Father and was revealed to us" (1 John 1:2). In what way, then, is Jesus "eternal life?" The answer is, Jesus is the way by which we receive eternal life, and He is the one with whom we spend it.

The subject of eternal life is prominent in the Gospel of John, showing us how eternal life was in Jesus, and how Jesus delivered it to us through His incarnation (becoming a man), earthly life, sacrificial death, and victorious resurrection. Note these verses which are among many in John's gospel that discuss eternal life:

Life was in Him [Jesus], and that life was the light of men. (John 1:4)

For God loved the world in this way: He gave His One and Only Son, so that everyone who believes in Him will not perish but have eternal life. (John 3:16)

But whoever drinks from the water that I will give him will never get thirsty again — ever! In fact, the water I will give him will become a well of water springing up within him for eternal life. (John 4:14)

I assure you: Anyone who hears My word and believes Him who sent Me has eternal life and will not come under judgment but has passed from death to life. (John 5:24)

A thief comes only to steal and to kill and to destroy. I have come so that they may have life and have it in abundance. (John 10:10)

I give them eternal life, and they will never perish — never! (John 10:28)

Jesus told him, "I am the way, the truth, and the life. No one comes to the Father except through me." (John 14:6)

This is eternal life: that they may know You, the only true God, and the One You have sent — Jesus Christ. (John 17:3)

The previous verse is particularly important. In it, Jesus defines eternal life as knowing —personally, relationally, and intimately — "the only true God, and the One You have sent — Jesus Christ" (John 17:3). First and foremost, then, the "eternal life" that God "gave" us in 1 John 5:11 is the opportunity to know His Son, Jesus Christ, through a personal relationship.

There is, to be sure, a future dimension to this eternal life, namely, an everlasting experience of life with Jesus. Scripture clearly declares that we will spend eternity —forever, without end — reigning over the universe with Christ. John refers to this dimension of eternal life in Revelation 22:5: "Night will no longer exist, and people will not need lamplight or sunlight, because the Lord God will give them light. And they will reign forever and ever." Although no living person has actually seen God — the Bible says no one can see God and live (Exodus 33:20) — all who believe in Him will live forever in His eternal kingdom. Eternal life, then, on the one hand, is a past reality manifest in the incarnate Son, and, on the other hand, a future promise of life with the Lord. It is a gift from God. He is its source.

Questions to Consider

According to John 5:24, when does eternal life begin? How does this affect your life?

The Cornerstone of Salvation: Christ

The heresy John is addressing in 1 John centers not only on the source of salvation, which is God, but also the exclusivity of salvation through Jesus Christ. John states, "The one who has the Son has life. The one who doesn't have the Son of God does not have life" (1 John 5:12). Simply put, according to Scripture, eternal life can only be received through Jesus Christ.

John also teaches the exclusivity of salvation through Jesus Christ in his gospel. Notice again John 14:6: "No one comes to the Father except through me." Here, John is reaffirming what he already stated earlier in John 3:36: "The one who believes in the Son has eternal life, but the one who refuses to believe in the Son will not see life; instead, the wrath of God remains on him." There is no access to heaven without a vital, life-changing relationship with Jesus. The two cannot be separated.

As our substitutionary sacrifice, Jesus paid the price for our salvation. After His earthly work was completed, He ascended into heaven, where He now intercedes for us before the Father (Hebrews 7:25). The New Testament describes Jesus as our Bridegroom (Ephesians 5:25-33; Revelation 19:7-8) and our Brother (Hebrews 2:11-18), further affirming that eternal life and heaven are a relationship with Him. Eternal life is not just about spending forever in Paradise; it's about spending forever with the One who created you. Further, to refuse such an offer is to face eternal separation from God (John 3:16). We must believe in the Son in order to have eternal life either now or after we die, but it will be too late. There is no other option. You will bow the knee to Him today as Savior, or you will bow the knee to Him as Judge at the judgment. Regardless, everyone will bow the knee to Him (Philippians 2:9-11).

Question to Consider

According to John 10:27-30, how can a believer be sure he or she has eternal life?

I'm Sure of My Salvation

It is upon the two truths above—the source of salvation in God and the cornerstone of salvation in Christ — that John establishes the security of the believer. He states in 1 John 5:13: "I have written these things to you who believe in the name of the Son of God, so that you may know that you have eternal life." In this verse, John plainly states his reason for penning this letter. 1 John was written that we may know—absolutely and without doubt—that we have eternal life. It is a guide by which we can evaluate our standing before a holy God.

Throughout this letter John teaches, on the one hand, that those who believe in the Son of God are heaven-bound. As a result of one's relationship with Jesus, believers will "walk in the light" (1 John 1:5-7), "obey God's commandments" (1 John 2:3-6; 3:24), "overcome sin" in their lives (1 John 3:3-9), and "love one another" (1 John 2:9-11; 3:11-23; 4:7-12). On the other hand, John makes it crystal clear that those who fail to practice these virtues do not have a relationship with Jesus. They, along with those who deny that Jesus is God, are walking in darkness far from Jesus.

When you compare your life to the teachings of 1 John, you will gain confidence of what genuine salvation looks like. John didn't say, "that you may *hope* that you have eternal life." He said, "that you may *know* that you have eternal life."

As you develop a deeper understanding of eternal life, be careful not to misconstrue the role of works in salvation. Although the Bible clearly teaches we are not saved by works (Galatians 2:16; Ephesians 2:8-9), we can gain assurance of our salvation by evaluating our works (which will be discussed in the next chapter). Our works merely stand as the proof that our lives have been gloriously changed by God's redeeming, purifying grace (Ephesians 2:10). Like evidence used to construct a case in a court of law, your life will be the convicting evidence to prove whether or not you are a believer or an unbeliever. We are not saved by works at all; we are justified by them (James 2:14-26). *Fruit is not the saving measure of salvation, but rather it is the evidence of a healthy, firmly-planted believer.*

Bear Bryant, the University of Alabama's legendary football coach, once sent a second-string quarterback into a game with instructions to run out the clock. After two successful plays, the quarterback threw a pass that was intercepted by an All-American safety. The quarterback, who was the slowest player on the field, dashed furiously toward the safety as he sprinted toward the end zone, catching him on the one-yard line. After the game, the opposing coach asked Bryant, "How in the world did your quarterback catch one of the fastest safeties on our team?" The legend replied, "Well, coach, it's like this. Your boy was running for six points, my boy was running for his life." [4]

The good news is, you don't have to run for eternal life! You don't have to do anything to earn it. If you believe in Jesus, you have eternal life. As long as you have accepted by faith the gift God offers to you through the death, burial, and resurrection of Jesus, you have all the assurance you will ever need!

Points to Ponder

*After reading this chapter, do you
believe God fully accepts you?*

If so, on what basis?

Chapter 2

How Can I Be So Sure?

Three Marks of a Believer

Over the past decade, I have witnessed personally the crippling effects of believing that a follower of Christ can lose their salvation. Those I observed were not unbelievers carelessly living like the world, but faithful Christians who wept repeatedly over staying in right standing with God. Their service for Christ was ineffective, and the fire of their salvation was doused by a spirit of doubt that clutched them in its paralyzing grip. Does the Bible assure us of our salvation? Where can we find confidence that we have eternal life? In the previous chapter we discussed the nature of salvation, showing how God is the source of salvation and Jesus is the cornerstone of salvation. In this chapter we continue to build upon this firm foundation by showing how our security in Christ rests upon three biblical truths: the promises of God's Word, the witness of God's Spirit, and the evidence of a changed life.

The Promises of God's Word

While H. A. Ironside was pastor of Moody Memorial Church in Chicago, an elderly man confessed his desperate struggle with the assurance of his salvation. He longed for some definite proof of his conversion, feeling that something tangible would solidify his faith in Christ. "Suppose," Ironside said to the man, "that you had a vision of an angel who told you your sins were forgiven. Would that be enough to rest on?" "Yes," the man replied, "I think it would. An angel should be right." Ironside proceeded, "But suppose that, on your deathbed, Satan came to you and said, 'I was that angel, transformed to deceive you.' What would you say?" The man was at a loss for words. Ironside explained that God has given us something more reliable and authoritative than the voice of an angel: He has given us His Son, who died for our sins and rose from the dead. Also, He has given us His written Word.

Ironside then read 1 John 5:13, "I have written these things to you who believe in the name of the Son of God, so that you may know that you have eternal life," before asking the doubter a question that each of us needs to answer: "Isn't that enough to rest on?"[5]

Ironside expressed the same confidence in the written Word that the biblical authors displayed. Peter wrote of his life-altering experiences with Jesus, specifically, witnessing the transfiguration. He states: "And we heard this voice when it came from heaven while we were with Him on the holy mountain. So we have the prophetic word strongly confirmed. You will do well to pay attention to it, as to a lamp shining in a dismal place, until the day dawns and the morning star rises in your hearts" (2 Peter 1:18-19). One might think an eyewitness of such an epic event would boast in the experience. Instead, Peter declares that the testimony of Scripture is more reliable than what he had seen with his own eyes!

Armed with such confidence in the Bible, the holy book that preserves the truth about the gospel, the Savior, and the salvation He provided for us, we can have full assurance of our salvation. We can trust that the Bible accurately preserves the words of Christ who claims:

My sheep hear My voice, I know them, and they follow Me. I give them eternal life, and they will never perish — ever! No one will snatch them out of My hand. My Father, who has given them to Me, is greater than all. No one is able to snatch them out of the Father's hand. The Father and I are one. (John 10:27-30)

Further, we can trust Paul, the Christ-commissioned messenger of the gospel, who confidently states:

Who can separate us from the love of Christ? Can affliction or anguish or persecution or famine or nakedness or sword? As it is written: Because of You we are being put to death all day long; we are counted as sheep to be slaughtered. No, in all these things we are more than victorious through Him who loved us. For I am persuaded that not even death or life, angels or rulers, things present or things to come, hostile powers, height or depth, or any other created thing will have the power to separate us from the love of God that is in Christ Jesus our Lord! (Romans 8:35-39)

Did you notice the impenetrable protection of God? Seventeen obstacles in these verses pose a threat to believers. Yet, not one of them has the power to separate you from Christ!

Points to Ponder

*Think about the fact that **nothing** can separate you from the love of God that is in Christ Jesus our Lord! What difference does that make in your life?*

Build Your Faith on Facts

A close friend of mine is one of the godliest men I know. He prays faithfully, regularly shares his faith with unbelievers, and actively makes disciples. For years, the lack of discipleship in his life and false teaching combined to produce a paralyzing fear that he would lose his salvation. In the early days of our praying together, he would repeatedly beg God, "Lord, do not take your Holy Spirit from me. Help me to know that I am saved. Give me assurance, Lord."

I continually encouraged him, but my comforting words fell on deaf ears. After years of counseling him, I finally said, "Listen, unbelievers don't ask the questions you are asking. Because they love their sin and have no desire for God, they don't ask questions about God. But you do! Your unquenchable desire to know that you are saved proves that you have been genuinely born again! The Bible says, 'Everyone who calls upon the name of the Lord will be saved.'" Victory finally came when he willfully conquered his feelings of doubt and chose to believe the promises of God's Word.

Author Christopher Adsit refers to this process as the "The Experience Bomb." He compares the Christian life to a train:

The engine car, "Fact," represents what we know to be true on the basis of the Word of God. The coal car, "Faith," represents our beliefs, our confidence in certain truths, which leads to opinions and actions. When we say we have faith in something, we are saying we believe it to be absolutely true, and we are willing to take action based on that belief. If I say I have faith that a certain chair will hold me up, I won't hesitate to sit down on it. The caboose, "Feelings," represents our subjective, emotional sensitivities and impressions. The train will run with or without the caboose, but it goes nowhere without the engine. Also, the train moves only if you shovel coal from the coal car into the engine. In the same way, our Christian lives will move only if we place our faith in the facts of God's Word. Now, as the engineer, you could hop up into the caboose and start hollering, "OK! Let's get this train moving! Start shoveling that coal back into here! Fire up this caboose and we'll get rolling! C'mon everybody, SHOVEL!" Just as the caboose has no ability to power a train, so your feelings have no ability to empower or direct your life as a Christian. It doesn't matter how much faith you put in your feelings, they won't get you anywhere.[6]

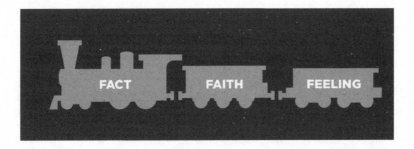

Figure 1[7]

Feelings are fickle, constantly fluctuating like the weather. Your faith must be based on the facts of God's Word, not on your constantly-changing emotions. The real issue for believers who lack assurance of salvation is a misunderstanding of their identity in Christ (we will discuss identity at length in Chapter 3). Declaring who we are in Christ reminds us that we...

- have been adopted into the family of God
- are joint heirs with Jesus
- have been redeemed and forgiven
- cannot be separated from the love of God
- are sealed with the promised Holy Spirit

I encouraged my friend to read a "Faith Declaration" based on the book of Ephesians every morning (see Appendix 1). The change in my friend's life was significant. By reciting Scripture to himself, he drowned out the spiritually-crippling influences that had plagued him for years.

Three negative voices — the world, the flesh, and the devil — disparage us every day. Therefore, we must constantly preach to ourselves the promises of God. Remind yourself daily, even repeatedly throughout the day, *whose* you are and *who* you are in Christ.

- → Are you claiming the promises of God?
- → Are you trusting in the finished work of Christ to save you?
- → Are you leaning on the facts of the Word of God?
- → You should be!

God does not deal in doubt and confusion, but in clarity and peace (1 Corinthians 14:33). Doubt surfaces from Satan and from within through unbelief (James 1:5-8). When you doubt or question what God has done in your life, rest in His Word, not on your feelings. Your feelings will eventually fail you; God's Word never will. When you doubt your salvation, you doubt the integrity and omnipotence of God!

Questions to Consider

Is it wise to let your faith be driven by your feelings? What should our faith rest upon?

The Witness of the Spirit

Scripture teaches that the moment you received Christ as Savior, you were <u>sealed</u> with the Holy Spirit. Paul states in Ephesians 1:13-14:

> *When you heard the message of truth, the gospel of your salvation, and when you believed in Him, you were also <u>sealed</u> with the promised Holy Spirit. He is the down-payment of our inheritance,*

for the redemption of the possession, to the praise of His glory (emphasis added).

In New Testament times, a seal was an official mark that was placed on a letter, contract, or important document to identify its sender, guarantor, or owner. A seal was formed when a signet ring was dipped in hot wax and then pressed into a document. From that moment on, the record was guaranteed by the owner of the signet. It could not be undone. In the same way the presence of God's Spirit in our lives is the seal of our salvation. This sealing of the Spirit has several characteristics.

First, the seal of the Spirit at salvation is *permanent.* In the Old Testament, the Holy Spirit had what is sometimes referred to as a "come and go" ministry, empowering individuals for a specific task and retreating after His work was done. Now, under the New Covenant initiated by the death of Christ, the Holy Spirit permanently indwells every believer, validating our relationship with God. He does not take up residence in our lives and then move out after a season. He resides with us the rest of our lives.

Second, the seal of the Spirit at salvation is *holistic.* At the moment of salvation, we received *all* of the Holy Spirit. The Spirit is not merely some power or force that is distributed incrementally. He is the Third Person of the Trinity who settles completely within us once and for all. To suggest otherwise is illogical. Because He is a person (by person I do not mean a human, but a Divine Being, and not merely a force or influence), either the Holy Spirit lives within us or He does not. Part of the Holy Spirit cannot live in you any more than part of you can live in the United States and the rest of you can live in China! Saying that we receive the Spirit in increments or phases reduces Him to being merely God's power and not the Third Person of the Trinity.

Third, the seal of the Spirit at salvation is *essential.* Because the spiritual birthmark of every believer is the indwelling Spirit of God, you cannot be saved without having the Holy Spirit. Scripture clearly states, "You, however, are not in the flesh but in the Spirit, since the Spirit of God lives in you. But if anyone does not have the Spirit of Christ, he does not belong to Him" (Romans 8:9). If you don't have the Spirit, you aren't saved. But if you do have the Spirit, you are saved. The seal of the Spirit represents God's ownership of you and His authority over you. You are secure because you belong to Him. When you received Christ, He purchased you with His blood that was shed at Calvary. The Holy Spirit is the evidence — the receipt or record — of that heavenly transaction.

Questions to Consider

We shouldn't doubt our salvation; however, is it important to examine whether we're in the faith? (2 Corinthians 13:5). What are ways to test our faith?

Evidence of a Changed Life

The Bible illustrates the transformation that takes place in the believer in a variety of ways. Paul, for example, refers to the converted believer as a "new creation": "Therefore, if anyone is in Christ, he is a new creation; old things have passed away, and look, new things have come" (2 Corinthians. 5:17). Another common image is a fruit-bearing tree. In Matthew 12, the Bible records Jesus' healing of a demon-possessed man. In response to the multitudes who were amazed by the miracle, the Pharisees accused Jesus of operating in the power of Satan. Jesus rebuked them by pointing to a simple fact of nature: "A tree is known by its fruit" (Matthew 12:33). The fruit of our lives — our words and deeds — reveal what kind of people we are. A tree that bears apples is an apple tree. A tree that produces pecans is a pecan tree. A person who practices righteousness is a believer. A person who *consistently* lives unrighteously has not been born again. A believer bears good fruit and an unbeliever bears bad fruit.

Simply put, the fruit of one's life identifies the root of one's heart.

The marks (or fruit) of one's life are revealing. First, the marks can identify those who are lost. John the Baptist preached that people whose fruit is consistently bad are subject to divine judgment. "Even now the ax is ready to strike the root of the trees! Therefore, every tree that doesn't produce good fruit will be cut down and thrown into the fire" (Matthew 3:10). The forerunner of the Messiah bluntly warned that those who do not repent, turn from sin towards God, and live righteously will be destroyed. Unrighteous words and deeds are a sign that an individual is lost and will spend eternity separated from God in hell.

Second, good fruit can identify those who are truly converted and give believers confidence that they are heaven bound. You can receive assurance of your salvation by examining your attitudes and actions. Your conduct proves your conversion. You don't justify your salvation by the date you were saved in the front of your Bible. *You justify your salvation by the conduct of your life.* A changed life affirms that your profession of faith in Christ was genuine. You are in Christ, and Christ is in you, producing good works.

As discussed in the previous chapter, the First Epistle of John was written to assure believers that they have eternal life. John's case for the genuine believer is built by presenting five evidences of those who have truly been born again. These traits are often called the birthmarks of the believer. First, those who have been saved will desire to tell others about Christ. This desire motivated John to write his account of Jesus' life and his epistles: "What was from the beginning, what we have heard, what we have seen with our eyes, what we have observed and have touched with our hands, concerning the Word of life — that life was revealed, and we have seen it and we testify and declare to you the eternal life that was with the Father and was revealed to us — what we have seen and heard we also declare to you, so that you may have fellowship along with us; and indeed our fellowship is with the Father and with His Son Jesus Christ" (1 John 1:1-3).

Are you burdened by the lost condition of those around you? Do you truly long to see people saved? Do you realize the explosive power in the message of the gospel? Are you troubled for lost friends and family? If not, it is evidence that you may not be saved. How can a person who possesses eternal life have little or no concern for those who are perishing around them?

Second, a genuine Christian will have a growing intimacy with other believers: "If we say, 'We have fellowship with Him,' yet we walk in darkness, we are lying and are not practicing the truth. But if we walk in the light as He Himself is in the light, we have fellowship with one another, and the blood of Jesus His Son cleanses us from all sin." (1 John 1:6-7). Christ did not cleanse us that we might walk in the light alone. We were cleansed (made holy) to constitute a holy community, one united in the worship and service of Christ. Do you long to fellowship with the body of Christ? Are you eager to share scriptural insights with other believers? Are your closest friends believers? Do you love learning new truths from other disciples of Christ?

Third, a true believer will sincerely desire to obey God: "This is how we are sure that we have come to know Him: by keeping His commands. The one who says, 'I have come to know Him,' yet does not keep His commands, is a liar, and the truth is not in him" (1 John. 2:3-4). Believers do not obey God accidentally or unintentionally, but on purpose. Do you consciously live out God's instructions as revealed in His Word? Do you view the commands of God as oppressive restrictions or as expressions of His love? Does your life line up with the Word?

Fourth, along with a growing love for the community of Christ-worshippers, a genuine believer will develop an increasing hatred for the world:

> Do not love the world or the things that belong to the world. If anyone loves the world, love for the Father is not in him. For everything that belongs to the world — the lust of the flesh, the lust of the eyes, and the pride in one's lifestyle — is not from the Father, but is from the

world. And the world with its lust is passing away, but the one who does God's will remains forever. (1 John 2:15-17)

Our world system is in stubborn rebellion against God and the gospel. Do worldly things attract you or distract you from your relationship with God? Do you love money, property, cars, sports, technology, art, shopping, fishing, or hunting more than you love God? I'm not saying we can't enjoy these things, but have they become an obsession in your life? Do they hinder your giving and service to the Lord? Do you find yourself laughing and being entertained by the things that break the heart of God? What do the movie ticket stubs in your pocket glorify? What about the music you listen to in your car? What about the history on your web browser?

Fifth, real Christians grow increasingly aware of their sin and desire righteousness, progressively gaining victory over the sin in their lives: "The one who commits sin is of the Devil, for the Devil has sinned from the beginning. The Son of God was revealed for this purpose: to destroy the Devil's works" (1 John 3:8). Does this verse imply that if you are in bondage to a habitual sin, a stronghold of Satan in your life, that you are not saved?

John MacArthur, author and pastor, explains the difference between Christians who try to live rightly but sin often, and non-believers who carelessly live in habitual sin:

I frequently receive letters from anguished Christians who doubt their salvation because they can't seem to break a sinful or unwise habit. They most often write about smoking, overeating, or pornography. They fear their struggle with such things means they are locked into a pattern of sin. But John is not saying that the frequent occurrence of one particular sin in a person's life means that person is lost.... A person who rejects God's authority doesn't care what God thinks about his habits, and is obviously not a Christian. A Christian however, has a drastically different way of relating to God. A true Christian can still sin, and may even do so frequently, but sinning frequently is not the same as practicing sin. In 1 John we see that a true believer can do the first, but not the second.[8]

Is sin a pattern in your life? Are you constantly taking an inventory of your sins? What are you doing to put to death the deeds of the flesh? Are you convicted because of your sins or are you calloused to them? Do you make excuses to justify your sinful acts or do you readily confess them, even though it might be painful? Do you sincerely desire to gain victory over them, or do you guiltlessly continue to commit them?

When people ask me, "Am I saved, Pastor?" My answer is, "I don't know. Time will tell." Adrian Rogers, former pastor of Bellevue Baptist, said, "A faith that fizzles before the finish had a flaw from the first."[9] I would add that a faith built on the foundation of Christ will continue to the end. The Apostle Paul said, "I have fought the good fight, I have finished the race, I have kept the faith" (2 Timothy 4:7). I am not implying that you will never be inoculated from sinning. We all sin. As long as we remain in these bodies, we will battle our fallen nature. Enticed by the attractiveness of the world and the desires of the flesh, believers can be led astray. But eventually a genuine believer will return to God. True repentance for a Christian is inevitable; true repentance for an unbeliever is impossible until he or she turns to Jesus. If you are unsure of your salvation, repent of your sins and put your faith in Christ today!

Don't Hope So, Know So

So, are you saved, sure, and secure, or are you scared, unsure, and insecure? God doesn't want you to have a "hope so," "guess so," or "think so" perspective on salvation. He wants you to "know so"!

Be sure that you know you have eternal life. Jesus says in John 5:24: "I assure you: Anyone who hears My word and believes Him who sent Me has eternal life and will not come under judgment but has passed from death to life." Do you believe this? Do you accept it as truth? Jesus' words give a "know so" view of salvation.

You don't have to feel it — feelings come and go. You just have to believe it. I pray that you will plant your feet upon this promise and say, "Yes, from this moment, I will know — without doubt — that I am a Christian!"

Don't read on without coming to this conclusion. If you don't have the assurance of your salvation, you will be hindered from having a growing relationship with God, for every time you are engaged in life's battles the enemy will whisper, "You aren't saved. You are fooling yourself." Are you standing on the promises of Scripture? Do you have the witness of the Holy Spirit in your life? Are you different than you were before you were saved? If so, firmly plant yourself in the clear teaching of God's Word, the firm declaration that you have been born again.

Points to Ponder

What are some evidences or birthmarks of a true believer? Are these birthmarks evident in your life?

Chapter 3

Dress for Success:

Our Identity in Christ

In our attempt so far to describe a firmly-planted believer, we have established the nature of salvation, showing how God is the source of salvation and Jesus is the cornerstone of salvation (Chapter 1). We continued to build upon that foundation by showing how one's assurance of salvation rests upon the promises of God's Word, the witness of God's Spirit, and the evidence of a changed life (Chapter 2). In this chapter we will discuss how the evidence of a changed life, that is, a believers' outward appearance or behavior, is a direct result of their new identity in Christ.

In the business world you'll hear, "Dress for success!" as if looking the part somehow enables you to play the part. It's a cliché rooted in good intentions, for it encourages forward steps into the role you wish to play. While appropriate dress is important, our clothes do not reflect who we really are. I could suit up in a firefighter's gear, but that wouldn't make me a fireman. If I purchased a white lab coat and stethoscope and wore them all over Chattanooga, I would probably get a lot of strange looks (and my staff might suggest that I get a psychological evaluation), but I would not be a medical doctor any more than I am now. I could wear a puffy white hat and apron, but I promise you that you do not want to eat what I cook.

Firemen are qualified to wear their protective gear because they have been specially trained to control and extinguish fires. Doctors wear lab coats and carry stethoscopes around their necks only after completing the required studies and earning a medical license. Chefs don toques and uniforms after they have finished culinary school. In each case, their attire does not qualify them for their professions; it merely reveals what they are.

Similarly, the believer's spiritual attire reveals who they are or, better yet, *whose* they are — followers of Christ. The key to the victorious, abundant Christian life is knowing who you are in Christ and dressing the part. Many believers, however, never understand their identity in Christ, hindering them from becoming firmly planted in the Christian life. In Ephesians 4, Paul admonished the believers in Ephesus to stop acting like the world and suit up with spiritual attire as Christ-followers. In order for the believer's outward appearance, or behavior, to match the inward effect of conversion a Christian must: 1) embrace the fact that they have been given a new identity in Christ, 2) renounce their old manner of life, and 3) embrace their new manner of life.

Believers Have Been Given a New Identity in Christ

In Ephesians 4:17, Paul writes: "Therefore, I say this and testify in the Lord: You should no longer walk as the Gentiles walk, in the futility of their thoughts." Simply stated, Paul teaches that Christians should not live as unsaved people live, because they have been given a *new nature*. In Old Testament times, the *Gentiles* were outside of God's covenant with Israel. Jewish Christians in the early church sometimes used this term to refer to individuals who did not have a relationship with God through a relationship with Jesus Christ. When we believe upon and receive Christ, we are to walk, or live, differently than those who do not know Him, for Christ now inhabits our very being.

One particular aspect of being "Gentile" that Paul highlights is the notion of *futility*. Notice the phrase "futility of their minds" in the verse above. The Greek word for *futility* means useless, fruitless, and unprofitable. Therefore *futility of their minds* describes a way of thinking that results in wasting your life on that which is without real meaning. Examples of this are found throughout Scripture. Solomon described this lifestyle when he compared being obsessed with fame, fortune, honor, and power to "chasing the wind" (Ecclesiastes 1:14). In the New Testament, the Prodigal Son wasted his inheritance through what the Bible calls "loose" (NASB) or "foolish" (HCSB) living (Luke 15:13). It is a philosophy that leads people to squander their lives on that which is empty, fleeting, and without eternal value. As those having received a new identity, how should we then live?

Renouncing Your Old Manner of Life

Paul goes on to further explain the futility of an unbelieving mind as one characterized by both debased thinking and depraved living.

Debased Thinking

In Ephesian 4:18, Paul describes the characteristics of most of the citizens of Ephesus, stating: "They are darkened in their understanding, excluded from the life of God, because of the ignorance that is in them and because of the hardness of their hearts." Ephesus was one of the most immoral cities in the ancient world. Five centuries before Christ, Heraclitus referred to Ephesus as, "The darkness of vileness. Their morals were lower than animals and the inhabitants were fit only to be drowned."[10] In the first century A.D., the temple of Artemis (the Olympian goddess of the moon) was the epicenter of the city's wickedness. Marked by despicable practices and perverted rituals, this idolatrous shrine was largely responsible for the immorality that plagued the city. Additionally, it was a refuge for the most hardened convicts due to a quarter-mile area outside the temple complex that was designated as an asylum for criminals.[11] As long as they remained within the confines of the property, lawbreakers were protected from prosecution.

Little had changed when Paul penned his letter to the Ephesians. Most, if not all, of the believers in Ephesus, had been saved out of this culture, knowing well its pressures and temptations. The believers were starkly aware of the sin that surrounded them, but the unbelievers remained blind to their sinfulness. Spiritual blindness is worse than physical blindness. A man who lacks physical sight knows that he is blind and accepts it. *But a man who is spiritually blind is also blind to the fact that he is blind.* Totally corrupted by his sinful nature, his thinking is debased, but he doesn't realize it.

Depraved Living

Because of their persistence in sin, the hearts of unbelieving Ephesians — the very core of who they were — had become hardened to their depraved condition. Paul paints a picture of their current state: "They became callous and gave themselves over to promiscuity for the practice of every kind of impurity with a desire for more and more" (Ephesians 4:19). The Greek word for *callous* describes the dense calcification that forms over a break in a bone, a substance which becomes harder than the bone itself. It also speaks of the new, tough skin that grows over old, damaged skin. Simply translated, it means to cease to feel pain. People with calloused hearts are numb to spiritual matters. Because their hearts are hardened, they are inattentive to the voice of God and the truth of His Word. Feeling no conviction of their sin, they ignore God and face His certain judgment.

The people of Ephesus and Rome indulged themselves in whatever pleasures appealed to their fallen nature. They possessed a license to sin, and they flashed it often. Every imaginable lewd act was accepted. Amused by graphic violence, their celebrated games viciously pitted man against man or animal until one died gruesomely. They committed one obscenity after another without conscience. Because they were calloused to the seriousness of their sin, immorality was as familiar to them as breathing.

America today is not far from such depravity. The same moral degradation that marked Ephesus can be witnessed in the modern

United States. Founded on Christian values, the United States has given itself over to debased thinking and depraved living. Acts that were once despised — premarital sex, adultery, abortion, homosexuality, divorce — have become socially acceptable even in some churches. (I preached a ten part series on these topics accessible at: brainerdbaptist.org/truenorth.) America is proving again that *what one generation allows, the next generation accepts, and the next generation promotes.*

One way that God judges such depravity is by giving calloused sinners over to the full consequences of their rebellion against His laws. Paul pointed out this truth in his Epistle to the Romans:

> *Therefore God delivered them over in the cravings of their hearts to sexual impurity, so that their bodies were degraded among themselves. . . . This is why God delivered them over to degrading passions. . . . And because they did not think it worthwhile to acknowledge God, God delivered them over to a worthless mind to do what is morally wrong.* (Romans 1:24, 26, 28; emphasis mine)

The punishment for their sin is that He allows them to continue in it. The Old Testament account of Israel's exodus from Egypt illustrates this fact. Scripture notes that Pharaoh repeatedly hardened his heart against God's command to release the Jews (Exodus 8:15, 32; 9:34). Later, the Bible says that God hardened Pharaoh's heart (Exodus 11:10). After Pharaoh hardened his heart for some time, God turned him over to his own devices.

Like the ruler of Egypt, people who do not believe in Christ become increasingly numb to morality and godliness. Blind to their condition, nothing in them initiates a move toward the Lord. For this reason, every human needs a *new heart,* one that is responsive to God. The prophet Ezekiel anticipates this very thing, stating: "I will give you a new heart and put a new spirit within you; I will remove your heart of stone and give you a heart of flesh" (Ezekiel 36:26). The ultimate fulfillment of this prophecy comes when one is converted. At the moment of salvation, God performs spiritual heart surgery on us by removing our hardened hearts and replacing them with a new, soft heart that is sensitive to Him and feels the conviction of sin.

Paul delved into the depraved condition of unbelievers for a penetrating purpose: to remind us of what we were like before surrendering our lives to Christ. We carelessly sinned before our salvation because we had a heart condition. But now, after repenting and believing in the purifying work of Christ, we have no excuse for our disobedience. As believers, we have been given a new nature and manner for living!

Question to Consider

According to Ephesians 2:1-3, what does this passage say about those who are without Christ?

Embracing Your New Manner of Life

The catalyst that changes our minds and lives is *learning Christ*. Paul continues his teaching: "But that is not how you learned about the Messiah, assuming you heard about Him and were taught by Him, because the truth is in Jesus" (Ephesians 4:20-21). What does Paul mean by the phrase "learned about the Messiah"? Paul was not speaking of merely learning the facts about Jesus, but of learning to live the abundant life Christ modeled and died to give us. When we receive the salvation freely offered to us through Christ's death, burial, and resurrection, we enter into a relationship with Him.

Relational knowledge of Christ increases through the study of God's Word. As we study the Bible, the Holy Spirit reveals Jesus to us (John 14:26; 15:26; 16:14). Additionally, the Spirit enables us to understand His teachings. Through this process of learning

Christ, our lives are gloriously transformed as we continually remove the old self and put on the new self.

Off with the Old Self

According to Paul, the "old self" is our old way of living that springs from our sinful human nature, a life characterized by disobedience, rebellion, and sin. He states in Ephesians 4:22 that, like our first parent, Adam, we were dead in our trespasses and sins as a result of the fall. But upon accepting God's gift of salvation, we are made alive in Christ, who is the representative of a new way of living. Paul explained our depraved condition in the second chapter of Ephesians:

> *And you were dead in your trespasses and sins in which you previously walked according to the ways of this world, according to the ruler who exercises authority over the lower heavens, the spirit now working in the disobedient. We too all previously lived among them in our fleshly desires, carrying out the inclinations of our flesh and thoughts, and we were by nature children under wrath as the others were also. But God, who is rich in mercy, because of His great love that He had for us, made us alive with the Messiah even though we were dead in trespasses. You are saved by grace!* (Ephesians 2:1-5)

Putting off the old self and putting on the new self is like taking off and putting on outer garments. In fact, the Greek word translated as "put off" is the word used for taking off clothes. As believers, God commands us to *put off* the sinful acts of the old self in the same way we take off dirty clothes. In the early church, those being baptized took off their old clothes and put on new, white garments to symbolize this transformation.

As we learn Christ, we begin to strip off the filthy garments of our sinful nature. Paul elaborated on this process more fully in his letter to the Colossians:

Therefore, put to death what belongs to your worldly nature: sexual immorality, impurity, lust, evil desire, and greed, which is idolatry. Because of these, God's wrath comes on the disobedient, and you once walked in these things when you were living in them. But now you must also put away all the following: anger, wrath, malice, slander, and filthy language from your mouth. Do not lie to one another, since you have put off the old self with its practices and have put on the new self. You are being renewed in knowledge according to the image of your Creator. (Colossians 3:5-10)

Paul is encouraging the believers to rid themselves of every corrupt practice that was part of their former life. We accomplish this by continually repenting of our sins. When should a Christian repent of wrongdoing? Immediately after it happens.

The Christian life is a life of perpetual repentance. Repentance is a change of mind that results in a changed life. As Christ's Spirit works within us through His Word, our debased thinking is changed, and, as a result, our lives are transformed. This is what Paul was talking about when he said, "Don't copy the behavior and customs of this world, but let God transform you into a new person by changing the way you think" (Romans 12:2, NLT).

Imagine a high school football player. After a three-hour practice on a sweltering August day, he is covered in dirt and drenched with sweat, not to mention the aroma that accompanies a day on the field. Because football is a contact sport, he also bears the stench of his teammates! Would he take a long shower in the locker room, apply deodorant, brush his hair, splash on cologne and then put on the same foul-smelling uniform in which he practiced? No way.

You might say, "I would never do that either!" But that is *exactly* what a born again believer does when he or she reverts back to their old manner of life. Taking off the old self requires action on your part. You may have to change the places you frequent, the movies you watch, the music you listen to, the websites you visit, and the people with whom you associate. You may have to change your phone number, email address, or Facebook friends — things

I did upon leaving my drug past behind (Chapter 1 of *Growing Up* contains my testimony).

What needs to be removed from your life? What sinful tendencies from the past have crept back in? Have you reverted back to your old ways? If you profess that you are saved, you should live like it. Such a radical change requires constant effort and honest self-examination. We tend to be blind to our own faults. Therefore, you may need to humble yourself and ask your spouse, a trusted friend, or both to give you an honest appraisal of your life. Trust me, it may be revealing and emotionally painful, but their insights might expose caustic elements of your old self that need to be removed.

Question to Consider

*According to Ephesians 2:4-10, describe
the transformation that takes place
when someone is born again?*

Put on the New Self

God does not intend for us to go through life spiritually unclothed any more than He desires that we parade around physically naked. Upon instructing us to take off the old self, Paul immediately admonishes believers to be "renewed in the spirit of your minds; you put on the new self, the one created according to God's likeness in righteousness and purity of the truth" (Ephesians 4:23-24). Earlier in this same passage, Paul spoke about the darkness that plagues the minds of unbelievers: "They are darkened in their understanding, excluded from the life of God, because of the ignorance that is in them and because of the hardness of their hearts" (Ephesians 4:18). But a marvelous transformation occurs in us when we believe. Through our union with Jesus and the reception of His grace, God illuminates our darkened minds, enabling us to identify and understand His truth.

According to Paul, *the spirit of our minds* — our entire mental framework — is *renewed*. That is, as the Spirit works in our lives to change us, we put on the new self, and, therefore, think and act in a new manner. Professor John Eadie describes this change:

> *The change is not in the mind psychologically, either in its essence or in its operation; and neither is it in the mind as if it were a superficial change of opinion on points of doctrine or practice; but it is in the spirit of the mind; in that which gives the mind both its bent and its material of thought. It is not simply in the spirit as if it lay there in dim and mystic quietude; but it is in the spirit of the mind; in the power which, when changed itself, radically alters the entire sphere and business of the inner mechanism.*[12]

Eadie explains that the act of salvation is not just a psychological phenomenon, nor is it a feel-good by-product of human-constructed religious action. He points out that it is an action of the *soul,* that immeasurable, eternal quality of human beings through which they are connected to God! The soul-transformation that comes from a saving faith in Jesus Christ is not a passive decision, it's one that can, and will, change a person's life from the inside out. Jesus saves in real, measurable, and concrete ways — our lives can be the proof of that.

When Christ saved you, everything changed, including your way of thinking. Again, the word "repentance," which means changing one's direction, also involves adopting a new mindset — the mind of Christ (Philippians 2:5). Remember, belief drives behavior; a change of mind leads to a change of actions. ***When you begin to think like Jesus, you will soon begin to live like Jesus.***

Many years ago, when I was battling an alcohol and drug addiction, I blamed everyone around me for my shortcomings. Eventually, I identified the real problem — *I* was the problem. When I changed my outlook on life, my world changed. If a change in thinking in the natural realm alters our perception of the people, places, and things around us, how much more can a change of mindset in the spiritual realm revolutionize our perspective on who we are in Christ and what impact our lives can have for the Kingdom of God?

Paul said, "Put on the *new self.*" In this context, "new" is a change from evil to good by the Spirit of God. When we are saved, the Lord gives us a new nature and a new heart, which result in a new demeanor and a new outlook on life. A creature tainted by a sinful nature is transformed into a purified worshipper made into the image of Christ! But it's up to us to act like it. It's up to us to embrace our new calling. The renewing of your mind includes a new capacity for spiritual things. You become sensitive to God's voice, and you are able to obey His Word. God doesn't renovate your old, sinful life; He gives a brand new life. You are a new person. You are not what you used to be, *so start living like it!*

Paul wholeheartedly embraced this new identity and lifestyle, declaring, "I no longer live, but Christ lives in me" (Galatians 2:20). Every day we choose to either live under the *old* self or walk in the *new* self. Will you act like who and what you are, or will you conform to a worldly standard? Dallas Willard said, "As Jesus' disciple, I am his apprentice in kingdom living. I am learning from him how to lead my life in the Kingdom of the Heavens as he would lead my life if he were I."[13] If Jesus were an electrician, what kind of electrician would He be? If Jesus were an accountant, what kind of accountant would He be? If He were a father, lawyer, business owner, doctor, factory worker, how would He live?

Perhaps it is easier to think about this through a metaphor. Imagine being convicted for a crime and sentenced to a prison cell for the rest of your life. You spend every day staring at the four walls of an eight-by-twelve foot cell. Your freedom is gone. One day, the guard informs you that someone has agreed to serve your sentence for you. Consequently, you are free to go. The cell door is opened, and you can leave if you choose. You are a new person — one who is no longer captive. Would you stay in that cell a moment longer? Upon exiting, would you also want to know who served your sentence and why?

Sin and death held you captive, but another man, Jesus Christ, came forward and willingly took your punishment. One day, you heard the gospel, repented of your sins, and believed. At that moment, the spiritual chains that shackled you fell off and you were set free. You were translated from a sinner to a saint. You went from being a child of wrath to a child of God. You were no longer a prisoner in the eyes of God, but a citizen of the kingdom of heaven. It's up to you to walk as a free person. Do you keep returning to that cell of sin? Do you keep entering the bondage from which you have been liberated? Why would you do so when you are *free*?!

A Prison Experiment Gone Bad

In the summer of 1971, Dr. Phil Zimbardo, former president of the American Psychological Association, conducted an experiment that would forever change how we view or perceive identity. He enlisted a number of Stanford University students to participate in the experiment in the basement of one of the buildings. Researchers interviewed over 70 applicants with a series of tests to determine psychological issues, medical history, drug history, or past crimes. They wanted to ensure the mental and physical health of the applicants, so that the results of their experiment would be as accurate as possible. Twenty-four healthy students were selected from the U.S. and Canada.

At the outset, Dr. Zimbardo divided the participants into two groups — guards and inmates — by the flip of a coin. The project was short-lived because the experiment was called off as a result of the brutality of the guards. Immediately, they assumed the identity and authority of the role in which they were placed. "Our planned two-week investigation into the psychology of prison life," according to Dr. Zimbardo, "had to be ended prematurely after only six days because of what the situation was doing to the college students who participated. In only a few days, our guards became sadistic and our prisoners became depressed and showed signs of extreme stress."[14] Even though the students received no formal training or visited a prison prior to the experiment, each assumed the role they were given and exercised that authority in their life.

Initially, they were told who they were and then they acted accordingly. The Christian life is similar in that believers are given a new identity in Christ and should act accordingly. You are a child of the King (Romans 8:15, 23; Galatians 4:5; Ephesians 1:5). You are a joint heir with Jesus (Romans 8:17). You are an object of God's love (1 John 3:1). You have been adopted in the family of God (Ephesians 5:1) and have a place in Heaven waiting for you. You are a new creation in Christ (2 Corinthians 5:17).

You don't need the support of others to succeed. God has already affirmed you! If God be for you, who can be against you? (Romans 8:31). He who is in you is greater than he who is in the world (1 John 4:4).

What we believe about ourselves does not matter. We are fickle people who are easily carried away by our emotions. All that matters is what God, through Scripture, says about you. According to the letter of Ephesians, you

. . . have been blessed with every spiritual blessing (1:3).

. . . have been chosen before the foundation of the world (1:4).

. . . are holy and blameless (1:4).

. . . have been predestined and adopted in love (1:5).

. . . have obtained an inheritance in heaven (1:10).

. . . have been sealed with the Holy Spirit of promise (1:13).

. . . have been made spiritually alive together with Christ (2:5).

. . . have been seated in Christ in heavenly places (2:6)

. . . have been saved by God's workmanship, created in Christ Jesus for good works (2:10).

. . . have been brought near to God by the blood of Christ, and Christ Himself is your peace (2:13).

. . . have access to God through Christ (2:18).

. . . are no longer a stranger and alien, but a fellow citizen with the saints and a member of God's household (2:19).

. . . are a fellow heir and fellow member of the body of Christ and a fellow partaker of the promise in Christ Jesus through the gospel (3:6).

. . . have boldness and a confident access to God through faith in Christ (3:12).

In Chapter 4, Paul shifts from a believer's identity to action steps one should take. In other words, because of who you are in Christ, you should live this way:

I will walk in a manner worthy of the calling with which I have been called (4:1).
I will use my spiritual gifts in the work of service, to the building up of the body of Christ (4:12).
I will no longer walk as the Gentiles walk — in the futility of their mind (4:17).
I will lay aside the old self and put on the new self through the renewing of my mind (4:23).

Whose report will you believe? The lies of the world, the flesh, and the devil? Or the unparalleled truth of God's inerrant, everlasting, and unchanging Word? Thank God for your new identity. Stop believing the lies of the enemy. Take hold of the promises of God and appropriate them in your life. You are a new person in Christ, so start acting like it! You will never be firmly planted in the Christian life until you do.

Points to Ponder

*Read Ephesians 1:13-14. Journal through
this passage and notice what the Bible
says to those who are "in Christ".*

Chapter 4

United in Christ:

Overcoming Temptation

In the previous chapter, we established how the evidence of a changed life — that is, the believer's outward appearance or behavior — is a direct reflection of their new identity in Christ. In this chapter we will build upon this important truth by showing that not only are believers to be identified with Christ, but they are actually *united* with Christ if they both *recognize* and *reckon* their new relationship to Christ.

When Abraham Lincoln affixed his signature to what is now known as the Emancipation Proclamation, every slave in the United States of America was legally free. Yet even though it was law, personal freedom for the newly freed slaves did not come until three things happened: 1) he knew the act was signed; 2) he believed what the act meant; and 3) he acted upon what he believed. A slave could not be considered free until he recognized and embraced his new legal status. He would need to understand and admit something like the following: "I recognize this glorious emancipation as the truth because it was codified by President Abraham Lincoln himself. Since I believe it, I am going to walk right out of this place and no one is allowed to touch me. If they do, they will be penalized since all the authority of the presidency is behind me."

Paul describes a similar reality in Romans 6:1-13, showing how believers are freed from slavery to sin and raised to new life in Christ at the moment of salvation. But as we will see in this chapter, recognizing and reckoning this truth are two different things. *Reckoning* can be used as a financial term to describe the process of counting up and balancing money coming in and money going out. It carries the idea of establishing something by calculation. God desires for believers to count the cost of their salvation. It is also important to recognize who you are in Christ and reckon what you are becoming in Christ, because what you believe effects how you behave. As already mentioned, right thinking naturally leads to right living.

Who am I?

Paul begins his argument by combating critics who suggest that since God extends grace when one sins, then believers should just go on sinning to display God's glory. He states: "What should we say then? Should we continue in sin so that grace may multiply? Absolutely not! How can we who died to sin still live in it?" (Romans 6:1-2). Paul's opponents were taking God's grace as a license to do that which was evil (Jude 3), supposing that if God's grace covers sin, a hedonistic lifestyle could be enjoyed without consequence. To demonstrate the inappropriateness of this theory, Paul reminds his audience of the model a believer is supposed to resemble. In 2 Corinthians 5:17, he reveals that, through Christ, old things die completely and are replaced with new things. Since a believer is not just a collection of recycled old parts, he is to be held to the standard of something completely new. A believer should recognize three essential responsibilities that come with the new life they have received: 1) they are united with Christ; 2) they have been crucified with Christ; and 3) they are freed from sin.

You Are United with Christ

My parents bought a high-powered juicer in an attempt to begin eating healthier. They described how they could mix carrots, pineapples, blueberries, apples, broccoli, and cauliflower together into one healthy, nutritious drink. I know your mouth is salivating as you read this. As nourishing as this may be, I would much rather eat all these things separately. Yet once the ingredients are mixed in the juicer, there is no reverse button. You can't un-blend what you have blended because the individual chunks of carrots, apples, and broccoli have amalgamated into one new substance. In a similar way, once you are joined together with Christ, the process cannot be undone. The two separate individuals are now one. Notice what Paul claims in Romans 6:5: "For if we have been joined with Him in the likeness of His death, we will certainly also be in the likeness of His resurrection."

Christians are commanded to be baptized with water after salvation, for baptism by water is an outward display of an inward decision to follow Christ (Matthew 28:19). You identify yourself with Christ in His death and resurrection and commemorate your unity as one through the Spirit. You become blended together. His death becomes your death, and His blessings from the Father become yours as well.

Furthermore, baptism for followers of Christ mirrors the spiritual baptism that takes place at conversion, and so outwardly demonstrates their spiritual identification with Jesus. By baptism, you reveal to the world and to the believing community that you have conformed yourself to Jesus and that you have been given a new life to follow Him.

Question to Consider

*What are other ways we can identify
with Christ beside baptism?*

Have Been Crucified with Christ

Part of being united with Christ means that you have been crucified with Christ. "For we know that our old self was crucified with Him in order that sin's dominion over the body may be abolished, so that we may no longer be enslaved to sin" (Romans 6:6). Some have argued that Paul's reference to being crucified with Christ means believers must therefore put their bodies through physical torment like Christ experienced. However, the phrase "we know that our old self was crucified with him" is not a command but a declarative statement. Paul is not suggesting that we are to actively crucify the flesh, although we put to death the deeds of the flesh; rather, he is reminding us in this verse that it has already been done. When Jesus was buried, you were buried with Him. Your flesh has already been crucified. Paul is not challenging believers in this verse to mortify or crucify the flesh. Instead, he reminds believers they are identified with Christ in his death and resurrection.

Evan Hopkins, an English pastor involved in the Keswick Movement, summarized this powerful truth well. He said, "God has put our old man — our original self — where He put our sins on the cross of Christ. Knowing this, that our old man was crucified with him, the believer there sees not only that Christ died for him — substitution — but that he died with Christ — identification."[15] If, however, believers have died to sin and the body of sin has been destroyed, then how is it that believers can sin at all? Several observations will help bring clarity to this important question and, together, offer a foundational understanding of the relationship between sin and the believer.

First, it is important to understand the tension in Scripture between the "already, but not yet."[16] The kingdom of God is in the present age, for we are already beneficiaries of kingdom blessings. Yet the full experience of the kingdom will only be realized at the return of Christ. This is how Paul can say, "You have died with Christ, the old man has been crucified, the body of sin has been brought to nothing, and believers are free to walk in newness of life because of the resurrection of Christ," even though none of us have experienced the resurrection.

What the ESV translates "brought to nothing" should not be taken to imply that the body of sin has been "annihilated." The HCSB renders it as "abolished." Another way of thinking of it is "rendered powerless" (cf. The New Living Translation and The International Standard Version). Christ subjugated the mastery of sin over your life, but not its presence. We know that Paul is not talking about sinless perfectionism because the context prohibits such an interpretation: "We know that Christ, having been raised from the dead, will not die again. Death no longer rules over Him" (Romans 6:9); "therefore do not let sin reign in your mortal body, so that you obey its desires" (Romans 6:12); and "don't you know that if you offer yourselves to someone as obedient slaves, you are slaves of that one you obey—either of sin leading to death or of obedience leading to righteousness?" (Romans 6:16).

Samuel Bolton, a Puritan pastor, in his book *The True Bounds of Christian Freedom*, helps us here:

> *We still have the presence of sin, which are the stirrings and workings of corruptions. These make us to have many a sad heart and wet eye. Yet Christ has far freed us from sin; it shall not have dominion. There may be the turbulence, but not the prevalence of sin. There may also be the stirrings of corruption. A godly man may be more troubled with sin when it is conquered than when it reigned. Sin will still work, but it is checked in its workings. Sin is under command. Indeed, it may get advantage, and may have a tyranny in the soul, but it will never more be sovereign. I say, it may get into the throne of heart and play the tyrant in this or that particular act of sin, but it shall never more be as a king there. Its reign is over; you will never yield voluntary obedience to sin. Sin is conquered, though it still is within you.[17]*

Second, in light of the tension between the "already, and not yet," Scripture teaches that you are definitively freed from sin. "A person who has died is freed from sin's claims" (Romans 6:7).

Being free from sin's claims begins with the finished work of Jesus on the cross. It is through His death that we are not only justified before God, but also freed from sin's grip on our lives. In His death, we have life. In His death, we have freedom. Indeed, this is the great irony of the Christian life: death precedes life.

We are freed from sin by the death of Christ. "Set free" is a forensic or legal term that is translated "justified" fifteen times in the Epistle to the Romans. Here are a few examples:

For no one will be justified in His sight by the works of the law, because the knowledge of sin comes through the law. (Romans 3:20)

Therefore, since we have been declared righteous by faith, we have peace with God through our Lord Jesus Christ. (Romans 5:1)

Paul also uses the same word in Acts 13:38-39:

Therefore, let it be known to you, brothers, that through this man forgiveness of sins is being proclaimed to you, and everyone who believes in Him is justified from everything that you could not be justified from through the law of Moses.

To be justified, then, is to be legally declared righteous before God at the moment of salvation. It is to be spoken of in hindsight. Our justification is a present reality, but it should be seen as separate from the active process of sanctification. Those who have died with Christ have been declared legally innocent and have been given the ability to overcome the mastery (or dominion) of sin through the Spirit.

Third, in light of the tension between the "already, and not yet," not only are believers freed from sin through their death in Christ, but they will also live with Christ. "Now if we died with Christ, we believe that we will also live with Him, because we know that Christ, having been raised from the dead, will not die again. Death no longer rules over Him" (Romans 6:8-9). Paul switches from speaking of our death in Christ to referring to our life in Him. He moves from positional justification before a holy God to putting that freedom into practice. He transitions from explaining what Jesus has done *for* us to what God is doing now *in* us, while stressing our part in the process — obedience.

The very moment a believer turns his or her life over to the care of Christ, they are recipients of the greatest hope imaginable. They are filled with purpose, they are given a promise, and they have the above assurance they will one day live with Him. Importantly, the phrase "we will also live with Him" is a future tense promise. That is, we will one day live with Him for eternity. Since He was raised from the dead, He cannot die again. This also means we will not die either. As you remember, when Jesus died on the cross, we died vicariously with Him. Since we experienced His death, we will also receive His reward — resurrection.

Our Reckoning Becomes a Reality

Believers must not only *recognize* that they are united with Christ, they must further *reckon* this new relationship to Christ. "Therefore do not let sin reign in your mortal body, so that you obey its desires. And do not offer any parts of it to sin as weapons for unrighteousness. But as those who are alive from the dead, offer yourselves to God, and all the parts of yourselves to God as weapons for righteousness" (Romans 6:12-13).

There was a children's book written a number of years ago called *The Treasure Tree,* by Dr. John Trent, in which four animals overcame various obstacles to find a tree full of precious treasures. Once they arrived at the gate guarding the tree, they noticed that there was something quite amiss. It required a very oddly shaped key to unlock it. Some were dismayed while others were excited about the possibility of adventure; nevertheless, they set out on a journey to find this strange key. They discovered that the key had four pieces, which were scattered about and guarded by cunning traps and creatures in need of help. What made the retrieval interesting, however, was that each of the four animals had something special about their personalities that made them perfectly suited to acquire one of the four pieces. It was not until they realized what their individual strengths were that they were able to work together to gather the pieces of the key and unlock the gate to the Treasure Tree.

This parable illustrates the concept of "reckoning." The animals in the story didn't *gain* anything, they instead just learned to understand and apply what they already possessed. In Romans, there is a shift from the indicative, the descriptive mood, to the imperative mood, which is used to extend a command: "So, you too consider yourselves dead to sin but alive to God in Christ Jesus . . . . [and] those who are alive from the dead, offer yourselves to God, and all the parts of yourselves to God as weapons for righteousness" (Romans 6:11, 13). Without a proper understanding of the original language, we can easily gloss over the meaning of these verses. There are two terms we need to examine closely: "consider" and "offer" or "present."

First, the Greek term translated "consider" is an accounting term. It means to carefully look over something and then to act upon what was observed. This verb is in the present tense, signifying an action that should be done daily, if not multiple times a day. For our purposes, let us associate this word *consider* with a word previously introduced: *reckon*. If your son comes to you and says, "I'm hungry," you might respond by saying, "Go to Burger King and purchase a meal." But if he had no money, he would respond by saying, "I can't, because I am broke." At that point, you may respond, "Yes you can. I deposited money in your account. Here is the slip printed out by the teller to prove it." If he then says, "I don't believe that," he fails to reckon it to be true. He didn't appropriate what was already in his account. His hunger and poverty would not be due to your failure to provide for him, it would be due to his failure to believe what you have already done for him.

When you came to Christ, you were blessed with all the spiritual resources of heaven. Notice how Paul illustrates this same truth in other passages:

We have also received an inheritance in Him, predestined according to the purpose of the One who works out everything in agreement with the decision of His will. (Ephesians 1:11)

When you heard the message of truth, the gospel of your salvation, and when you believed in Him, you were also sealed with the promised Holy Spirit. (Ephesians 1:13)

You do not receive the blessing of God incrementally, for He gave it in full when you came to Christ. God did not hold back from you, hence, you do not need a second blessing, as some mistakenly believe. Even though He gave us everything in Christ, we must appropriate or apply the resources of heaven to our life. Faith is laying hold of the promises of God and believing them. Appropriation is putting into action what you know by faith. In this way, truths sink in deep within your soul and give rise to righteous actions — belief drives behavior. Through His death on the cross, Christ paid the debt for our sins in full. Our old sinful nature was rendered inoperative; it no longer masters us.

Question to Consider

As you reflect on the difference between faith and appropriation, what are some examples of how you've seen this in your own life?

Augustine of Hippo, also known as St. Augustine, lived a promiscuous life before coming to Christ at thirty-one years of age. His book *Confessions* records his youthful excesses. Before becoming a priest, he fathered a child by a mistress. But his life radically changed in 387 A.D. when Ambrose, his spiritual father, baptized him. After conversion, he was seen by one of the mistresses from his former life. She called out: "Augustine, it is I. It is I!" Quickening his pace, he ran away from her while shouting over his shoulder, "Yes, but it is not I. It is not I!"[18] Augustine knew who he was before Christ, but moreover, he knew what he had become now in Christ. Augustine appropriated the truth of God's Word and acted upon it. *Believing Jesus died is history. Believing Jesus died for you is salvation.* That's a big difference.

Question to Consider

Why is "reckoning" important when overcoming temptation?

Next, it is important to understand the term "present" (Romans 6:13), which comes at the turning point of Paul's letter to the Romans. The word means, "to put at someone's disposal."[19] What Paul writes could read, "Do not let sin reign in your mortal body. Do not offer the parts of your body to sin but rather offer yourselves to God, and offer each member of your body to Him." Since we are slaves to God and not to sin, it makes sense to place ourselves at the complete disposal of the master.

When you read Romans 6:6, "We know that our old self was crucified with Him in order that the body of sin might be brought to nothing, so that we would no longer be enslaved to sin," your mind may jump to Galatians 5:24 where Paul writes, "Those who belong to Christ Jesus have crucified the flesh with its passions and desires." But the two verses are entirely different. Romans 6 speaks of what happened to us — our old self was crucified with Christ — while Galatians 5 refers to something we are expected to do — we are to crucify our sinful nature. *We are to die to sin once and for all, but we are to die to ourselves daily.*

Stuart Briscoe was drafted into the Royal Marines during the Korean War. He was assigned under a rigid Sergeant Major who strutted around the barracks placing burdens on his men. Briscoe did not realize how dominant this man had become in his life until the day he was released from the Marines. With release papers in hand, he was enjoying his newfound freedom by slouching a little and whistling aloud, which would have gotten him in serious trouble were he on duty. At that moment, Briscoe saw the Sergeant walking toward him. Impulsively, he jumped to attention without thinking, until he realized that he had died to this man. He was not dead, and neither was the Sergeant Major. But the Major's domination over his life had ended. He reckoned his newfound freedom, decided not to yield to his authority, and refused to raise his arms high and march in a single file line. Instead, he remained calm with his feet and hands by his side, as a former Marine. The sergeant could do nothing about it.[20]

Do you reckon your freedom to be true? When you are faced with temptation, do you respond to it as one who is dead to sin would? Do you remind yourself that you have been crucified with Christ and that you no longer live in the old pattern of life? Have you appropriated what has been credited to your account by acting like a new creature in Christ? Just like in the illustration of the soldier, we are dead to our former self and sin, and alive to Christ. Don't let sin control you anymore. *There are realities in the Christian life that you will never experience until you believe these truths and appropriate them to your life.*

Points to Ponder

*What may be stopping you from "recognizing"
and "reckoning" your union with Christ?*

How can you begin to change that today?

Chapter 5

A Walk to Remember:

Walking in the Spirit

Spiritual growth occurs, in part, through the transformation of the mind. To be sure, the firmly-planted believer will take action. But, as was stated earlier, right thinking drives right behavior. With this in mind, let's briefly review the core, foundational truths from the previous chapters: 1) God is the source of salvation and Jesus is the cornerstone of salvation, 2) the believer's assurance of salvation rests upon the promises of God's Word, the witness of God's Spirit, and the evidence of a changed life, 3) the born again believer has been given a new identity in Christ, and 4) the believer is united with Christ in such a way that he is free from his old self. In this chapter we will briefly examine the war that rages within every Christian, as well as the victory that can be yours as you learn to walk in the Spirit.

At the age of 35, I suddenly began experiencing disorientation, clouded thinking, and tingling sensations throughout my body. To determine the cause of these startling symptoms, my doctor ordered a battery of tests, including an electrocardiogram (EKG), an echocardiogram, a chest X-ray, extensive blood work, and a glucose tolerance test. Of all these procedures, I feared the final test most: the infamous stress test.

I dread cardio exercises. Embarrassingly, I must confess that I even drive my car to our church's community center, even though it is just across the parking lot from my office. Needless to say, the thought of intentionally induced stress on my heart did not excite me. The day of my doom all too quickly arrived. As the nurse prepared me, she explained what was about to occur. "Mr. Gallaty, we are going to monitor your heart as we raise its rate."

I confidently declared, "Ma'am, I should be fine. I actually pushed it really hard yesterday on a stationary bike to prepare for today's test."

"That's good," she smirked. "What did you get your heart rate up to?"

"160," I smugly boasted.

"That's a good start, but today our target is 187."

Upon hearing that number, I began to tremble and broke out in a cold sweat. Reaching a heart rate of 160 had stretched me to the limit. I stepped apprehensively onto the dreaded treadmill. During the next fifteen minutes, I exercised more strenuously than I had in nearly two decades. Starting with a slow walk at a moderate incline, the nurse gradually increased the intensity of the treadmill until I was fully jogging at a slope that rivaled Mount Everest. I was panting like a dog in chase; I was a *Survivor* song and a montage away from a Rocky Balboa movie. This grueling exercise was designed to reveal problems with my heart, but for me it revealed something else as well — I needed more exercise!

Doctors constantly tout the benefits of cardiovascular exercise. Even moderate amounts of it, like simply going for a walk, has tremendous life-lengthening benefits for our bodies. Similarly, the spiritual exercise of walking is crucial to our spiritual health, producing maturity, stability, and Christ-like character.

Walking in the Spirit, like walking for physical exercise, requires discipline, energy, and effort. But its payoff is enormous. Just as physical walking helps us overcome the enemies which threaten to destroy our health and shorten our lives, walking in the Spirit produces victory over our spiritual enemies — the world, the flesh, and the devil. To be firmly planted as a Christian, you must understand the war that rages between the flesh and the Spirit and resolve to deny the flesh and walk in the Spirit.

A Tactical Plan for Battle

In his Epistle to the Galatians, Paul described the conflict raging within every believer:

> *I say then, walk by the Spirit and you will not carry out the desire of the flesh. For the flesh desires what is against the Spirit, and the Spirit desires what is against the flesh; these are opposed to each other, so that you don't do what you want. But if you are led by the Spirit, you are not under the law. Now the works of the flesh are obvious: sexual immorality, moral impurity, promiscuity, idolatry, sorcery, hatreds, strife, jealousy, outbursts of anger, selfish ambitions, dissensions, factions, envy, drunkenness, carousing, and anything similar. I tell you about these things in advance—as I told you before—that those who practice such things will not inherit the kingdom of God. But the fruit of the Spirit is love, joy, peace, patience, kindness, goodness, faith, gentleness, self-control. Against such things there is no law. Now those who belong to Christ Jesus have crucified the flesh with its passions and desires. Since we live by the Spirit, we must also follow the Spirit* (Galatians 5:16-25).

One of the ways the Bible portrays the Christian life is as a walk. God sent Abraham on a cross-country hike. Moses led the Israelites on a forty-year walk through the desert. Joshua journeyed into the Promised Land. Jesus called to the disciples to follow — walk after — Him. The Christian life is a walk; that is, the sum total of your actions and attitudes. The question, then, is not *if* you are walking, for you are walking somewhere; the question is what path do you find yourself walking on? As a believer, you have two paths to follow: the way of the flesh or the way of the Spirit.

Questions to Consider

*Why do you think scripture uses the term "walk"
rather than "run or sprint?" How can you
adjust your life for a walk and not a sprint?*

Wandering in the Flesh

Consider again Paul's words in Galatians 5:16-17: "I say then, walk by the Spirit and you will not carry out the desire of the flesh. For the flesh desires what is against the Spirit, and the Spirit desires what is against the flesh; these are opposed to each other, so that you don't do what you want." Two important truths about the flesh emerge from this text. First, the flesh restrains your response to God's work. Second, the flesh reveals a heart alienated from God.

The Flesh Restrains Your Response to God's Work

When we are saved, Christ gives us a new, righteous nature. In order to walk in victory over sin, we must battle against our old, sinful nature. Our old nature is determined by our physical birth, but our new nature is something quite different — it is who we are according to our spiritual birth. According to Scripture, these two — the old and the new natures — are in constant conflict with one another. The Bible simply refers to these opposing natures as the "flesh" and the "Spirit." Neil T. Anderson defines the flesh as "learned independence." Consider his description below:

[Before salvation] you learned to live your life independent of God. This learned independence from God is a major characteristic of

54

what Scripture calls the flesh…. Flesh patterns don't just leave. They are slowly replaced or overcome as we renew our minds.[21]

Some Christians believe that when a person accepts Jesus as Lord and Savior, God eradicates their old nature. However, this is not what Scripture teaches. Biblical texts such as Romans 7:14-25, Galatians 5:16-25, Ephesians 4:17-32, and Colossians 3:5-14 teach that as we walk with Christ, our sinful nature becomes increasingly subdued. The old nature never disappears. You simply despise it and recognize your need to thrust it upon the cross of Jesus daily. We are at constant war with ourselves, and there is no hope for a ceasefire until we are delivered from these sinful bodies at death.

This truth becomes clearer when we study Paul's discourse in Romans. After outlining our salvation in Romans 5-6, Paul speaks of the battle raging in his body *as a Christian* (Romans 7). The frustration of succumbing to things that grieved his spirit — acts that his new nature despised — led him to exclaim: "What a wretched man I am! Who will rescue me from this dying body? I thank God through Jesus Christ our Lord! So then, with my mind I myself am a slave to the law of God, but with my flesh, to the law of sin" (Romans 7:24-25).

A firmly-planted faith is more than merely walking an aisle as a child, signing a membership card, or showing up every Sunday to sing to and hear from God. It is an intentional battle against the depraved nature of your former self. To pretend that your bout with sin or temptation is over is to both lie to yourself and diminish the outstretched hand of a Savior willing to fight by your side. While you are on this earth, you must live in this deeply flawed body until you die or Christ returns, whichever occurs first. The moment you let your guard down you will be defeated. The worldly wrapping of flesh around you restrains your worship of God and the expression of God's power through you.

Questions to Consider

If our old nature is at war with our new nature, then what should we anticipate as we seek to follow the Lord? What steps can we take to prepare for it?

The Flesh Reveals a Heart Alienated from God

In order for believers to identify the characteristics of walking in the flesh, Paul provides a non-exhaustive list of sins that spring from our unregenerated nature: "Now the works of the flesh are obvious: sexual immorality, moral impurity, promiscuity, idolatry, sorcery, hatreds, strife, jealousy, outbursts of anger, selfish ambitions, dissensions, factions, envy, drunkenness, carousing, and anything similar" (Galatians 5:19-21).

The first three sins — "sexual immorality," "impurity," and "sensuality" — are sexual in nature. The next two, "idolatry" and "sorcery," are associated with worshipping false gods. The next eight sins — "enmity," "strife," "jealousy," "fits of anger," "rivalries," "dissensions," "divisions," and "envy" — are commonly exhibited during social conflicts. The final two sins — "drunkenness" and "orgies" — stem from a lack of self-control. Paul had previously warned the Galatians about these particular sins along with the stiff penalty for committing them: "I tell you about these things in advance—as I told you before—that those who practice such things will not inherit the kingdom of God" (Galatians 5:21). How, then, can someone enter the kingdom of God if committing one of these sins disqualifies them?

Many have misused this passage to support the position that a believer can lose his or her salvation. Yet such an argument is disarmed by a careful examination of the Greek word "prasso," translated in English as "to do." If this word is misunderstood, it drastically changes the meaning of the verse. The Greek form of this word speaks of a repeated or continuous action. Hence, "to do" refers to the pattern of one's life — the whole of a person's actions — rather than a single, isolated act. Therefore, the continued, habitual, remorseless practice of sin identifies a person as having never genuinely repented and been saved.

Like all unbelievers, he or she will not enter the kingdom of God, not because the action has disqualified them, but because they never received the gift of salvation in the first place. John explained this in his first Epistle:

> *Everyone who commits sin also breaks the law; sin is the breaking of law. You know that He was revealed so that He might take away sins, and there is no sin in Him. Everyone who remains in Him does not sin; everyone who sins has not seen Him or known Him. Everyone who has been born of God does not sin, because His seed remains in him; he is not able to sin, because he has been born of God. This is how God's children — and the Devil's children — are made evident. Whoever does not do what is right is not of God, especially the one who does not love his brother.* (1 John 3:4-6, 9-10)

As fallen individuals, we will inevitably sin after we are saved. But indulging in a sin to the point that we become calloused to its toxic nature, or even start to condone its practice, proves that we are separated from God and have never truly been born again.

If you are reading this section with a fearful spirit, anguishing over a certain sin that is plaguing your life and wishing that you could be rid of such wickedness, then you are likely not the type of person about whom Paul and John wrote. By grieving over your sins and desiring to overcome them, you are proving to be truly repentant of your unrighteousness. Anyone desiring forgiveness from their sins will receive it.

The best response, however, is not to live in fear but to experience the joy of God's forgiving grace. Go before the Lord, confess your sin, ask His forgiveness, and pray that He will lead you away from temptation and deliver you from the evil one (Matthew 6:13). Pray for the power of His indwelling Spirit to give you victory over your fleshly desires.

As long as we are in these bodies, we are predisposed to sinning. But do not resign yourself to sin's power over your fallen nature. Walk in the victory Christ secured for us on the cross. Strive to be a person who is characterized by confession and thanksgiving rather than by the sinful pollution of the world.

Walking in the Spirit

Paul does not, however, leave his readers without a clear path on which to walk. "But if you are led by the Spirit, you are not under the law" (Galatians 5:18). Walking by the Spirit results in fruit of the Spirit.

Freedom in the Spirit

Living *under the Law* leads to a life of defeat, bondage, and spiritual ineffectiveness. The Judaic Law is incapable of saving us. It reveals our sinfulness before a holy God and confirms our deserving of God's judgment. Paul states earlier in Galatians:

> *Know that no one is justified by the works of the law but by faith in Jesus Christ. And we have believed in Christ Jesus so that we might be justified by faith in Christ and not by the works of the law, because by the works of the law no human being will be justified.* (Galatians 2:16)

The law condemns us; it cannot deliver us from sin.

Thus, freedom from the law does not mean that we can do as we please. Paul warned the Galatians about this: "For you were called to be free, brothers; only don't use this freedom as an opportunity for the flesh, but serve one another through love" (Galatians 5:13). As believers redeemed from the curse of the law, we are not allowed to live like the world. We are freed from the oppressive, hopeless bondage of the law to serve a kind, gentle, caring Master who offers us eternal life. You are no longer a slave to the eternal judgment that comes from a list of requirements you can never live up to. You are, instead, in love with the Savior who *did*.

Question to Consider

What is the danger in attempting to secure or validate your salvation through keeping the law?

Limiting our Liberation

Think of a dog that has been rescued from an animal shelter by a loving family who places him in the confines of a fenced yard. Is it cruel to rescue the dog from one form of captivity and place him in another? Absolutely not! By taking the dog home from the shelter, the family rescued him from impending death. By giving him boundaries, they are protecting him from the dangers that lie outside the fence. He is free to run and play and enjoy a safe life within the confines of the yard. Within the fence, he has food, water, and shelter. It does not limit his freedom; it preserves his life. Should the dog wander beyond his master's property he would no longer be truly free. He would be a prisoner to a world of fast moving vehicles, dogcatchers, limited food, and inadequate shelter.

Similarly, we were rescued from slavery under the law and brought into freedom under the shelter of the Spirit. God's commandments are our boundaries, but by no means do they keep us from being free; they protect our freedom and our lives. For example, God in His Word has instructed me not to steal. This command is not intended to limit my freedom, but to protect me from once again becoming a slave to sin. Should I choose to disobey God and steal, I will lose my freedom. I will be forced to keep knowledge of my sin away from my family, friends, and authorities, all the while being plagued by the fear of the consequences of my action. Additionally, I will be tormented by my guilty conscience, and convicted by God's indwelling Holy Spirit until I deal with my sin.

If caught stealing, I could face imprisonment for my actions. By ignoring my Master, Jesus, I would subject myself once again to the slavery of my former life instead of enjoying the freedom of my new life. How do you view God's commands? Are they restrictions to your happiness or expressions of His love for you? As a Christian, you have liberty, but liberty is not a license to sin. Adrian Rogers said, "Some people say, 'Well, if I believed in this doctrine, then I'd get saved and I'd sin all I want to.' Friend, I sin all I want to. I sin more than I want to. I don't want to! When you get saved you get your wanter fixed. As a matter of fact, you get a brand new wanter."[22]

Being led by the Spirit is more than God showing us the correct path to take or pointing out the right direction to walk. When the Spirit is leading you, He is the dominating influence in your life. He doesn't just reveal the way, He directs you in the way. He walks with you. We should respond to the Spirit's leading by surrendering our lives to His direction. Remember, the Holy Spirit is a person, the Third Person of the Trinity. He is co-eternal with the Father and the Son and is equal to them both. He is not a "thing" or an "it." He is a person. Submit to His direction, and allow Him to control your life.

Bearing Fruit That Remains

When we surrender to the Holy Spirit, our lives will bear the fruit of His control. In Galatians 5, the fruit of the Spirit is in sharp contrast to the works of our sinful flesh. "But the fruit of the Spirit is love, joy, peace, patience, kindness, goodness, faith, gentleness, self-control. Against such things there is no law" (Galatians 5:22-23). The first three virtues — "love," "joy," and "peace" — are habits of the mind that are generated from God. The following three acts — "patience," "kindness," and "goodness" — are virtuous deeds expressed to others. The final three — "faithfulness," "gentleness," and "self-control" — describe the general conduct of a believer.

Although Paul lists nine virtues, the word "fruit" is singular, signifying these qualities are unified and should *all* be found in believers, to some degree or another, who live under the Spirit's control. In essence, this "fruit of the Spirit" is simply the life of Christ lived out in a Christian. If we are bearing this fruit, then we are reflecting the very image of Christ.

We are not, however, responsible for producing this fruit. We can only exhibit these qualities in our lives by the power of God's Spirit. Even under the Old Covenant of Law, a believer could only produce good fruit by God's initiative. In Hosea, the Lord declared to Israel, "From Me comes your fruit" (Hosea 14:8).

Indeed, fruit provides evidence of our salvation. In the Sermon on the Mount, Jesus said, "You will know them by their fruit" (Matthew 7:16). *The fruit of one's life reveals the root of one's heart.*

Question to Consider

Why do you think that Scripture references "fruit" to describe the work of the Spirit?

Victorious Christian Living

There are two ways by which you can have victory over the flesh and walk by the Spirit: 1) remembering your past and 2) relying on the Spirit.

Remember Your Past

If you are a Christian, your flesh has already been crucified on the cross. Paul states in Galatians 5:24: "Now those who belong to

Christ Jesus have crucified the flesh with its passions and desires." When Jesus was crucified, you were hung on the cross with Him (Galatians 2:20). That means that when He died, you died. Was this a metaphorical crucifixion? By no means! It was an actual spiritual reality in your life. Here, Paul is challenging believers to mortify (put to death) the flesh by their own actions. Timothy George, in his commentary on Galatians, explains: "Believers themselves are the agents of this crucifixion. Paul was here describing the process of mortification, the daily putting to death of the flesh through the disciplines of prayer, fasting, repentance, and self-control."[23] Disciples of Christ "deny themselves, take up their cross, and follow him" (Luke 9:23).

Paul reminds believers to identify with Christ in His death — the penalty already served even for the sins you will commit tomorrow — and appropriate His finished work on the cross through faith. God subjugates our flesh through obedience to His commands. We have the gift of a Man who was better than death (for He was raised from it), more powerful than hell (for He won the keys to it), and who does not intend to keep it to Himself. Rather, He stands on the shore and says, "Follow Me!" It is our job to recognize this grace and to welcome it into our lives.

Our relationship with Christ crucifies the flesh, and it is by this relationship that we will experience His resurrection. Consider Romans 6:3-5:

> *Or are you unaware that all of us who were baptized into Christ Jesus were baptized into His death? Therefore we were buried with Him by baptism into death, in order that, just as Christ was raised from the dead by the glory of the Father, so we too may walk in a new way of life. For if we have been joined with Him in the likeness of His death, we will certainly also be in the likeness of His resurrection.*

When Christ died, you and I died on that cross. Therefore, since we have died with Christ, we will receive Christ's reward — a resurrected body and exaltation to the right hand of God (Revelation 3:21) — completely undeservedly. It is through our suffering and death with Jesus that the Christian paradoxically conquers all.

Point to Ponder

What are some areas in your life that have not been surrendered to Christ?

Rely on the Spirit

Living in the Spirit and *walking* by the Spirit are one and the same. Consider Paul's words in Galatians 5:25: "Since we live by the Spirit, we must also follow the Spirit." *Walking* in the New Testament does not refer to a collection of individual instances, but to a continuous, flowing movement. It stresses the journey itself rather than each step involved. Therefore, we can accurately define the command to *walk in the Spirit* as adhering to a Spirit-centered, Spirit-controlled lifestyle. It is aligning your compass in the direction of Christ and steering consistently, through doldrums and tempests alike, towards Him.

Similarly, the command to "live by the Spirit" refers to a life that continuously honors and follows God's indwelling Holy Spirit. The Greek verb "to live" refers to how a person conducts his or her life or how one behaves.[24]

When Paul wrote that we are to "live by the Spirit," he was saying that we should move with the ebb and flow of God's Spirit within us. As we walk through life by the Spirit, we are progressively growing as believers. We have no part in our justification — it is entirely the work of God — but we do participate in our sanctification, growing in holiness and becoming conformed to the image of Christ. As long as we yield to the Spirit, we are moving toward complete perfection at glorification, even though we will not receive complete perfection as long as the flesh exists. *Justification* freed us from the penalty of sin. *Sanctification* frees us from the power of sin. *Glorification* will free us from the presence of sin.

However, if we refuse to walk in the Spirit, we will continue to live in disobedience to God. Systematic Theology professor Wayne Grudem clarifies: "The New Testament does not suggest any short cuts by which we can grow in sanctification, but simply encourages us repeatedly to give ourselves to the old-fashioned, time-honored means: Bible meditation/memory, prayer, fasting, worship, fellowship with believers, evangelism, and self-discipline."[25]

You must always remember that the Christian life is impossible to live if you try to live it in your own strength. It becomes easier as you allow Christ to work in and through your life. "Easier," though, will never be "easy." Your battle is against the flesh. Expect sanctification to be a struggle, but always remember that you can be victorious over the flesh and sin by yielding to God's Spirit working in and through you, not by your own efforts. The following passages address the working of the Spirit over your own physical actions:

> So then, my dear friends, just as you have always obeyed, not only in my presence, but now even more in my absence, work out your own salvation with fear and trembling. (Philippians 2:12)

> For you are saved by grace through faith, and this is not from yourselves; it is God's gift — not from works, so that no one can boast. For we are His creation, created in Christ Jesus for good works, which God prepared ahead of time so that we should walk in them. (Ephesians 2:8-10)

> Now to Him who is able to do above and beyond all that we ask or think according to the power that works in us. (Ephesians 2:20)

Question to Consider

*What are ways to live the Christian
life in our own strength?*

An awesome, supernatural synergy occurs when we cooperate with God. We must work with Him, actively participating in all He wants to do in and through us. We are insufficient in and of ourselves for spiritual tasks, especially the grueling burden of overcoming the flesh (Isaiah 64:6). Without the strength and ability God gives, we are completely powerless. But when we merge our will with the leading of God's indwelling Spirit, we are empowered from on high. This supernatural power enables us to grow in holiness and conquer the flesh.

A group of nineteenth century pastors gathered to plan a citywide evangelistic campaign. One suggested inviting well-known evangelist D. L. Moody to bring the messages. As the ministers discussed the proposal, several spoke favorably about Moody. One young pastor opposed inviting Moody, sarcastically stating, "By the way some of you talk, you'd think Mr. Moody has a monopoly on the Holy Spirit." The room suddenly became quiet.

After what seemed like an eternity of silence, another pastor thoughtfully replied, "No, Mr. Moody doesn't have a monopoly on the Holy Spirit, but the Holy Spirit does have a monopoly on Mr. Moody!"[26] The pastor recognized that D. L. Moody was a man who had not only yielded his body to be a temple of the Holy Spirit but had learned to be fully submissive to God's will. No one has a monopoly on the Holy Spirit, but if you are going to walk in consistent victory over the flesh, He must have a monopoly on you.

Does He?

We need to begin each day by praying to the Lord, "Fill me with Your Spirit today so that I may do Your will." Do you begin your days by pleading for His assistance? Do you start every meeting by asking for His help? Do you pause for prayer before every decision? Have you spoken to Him today? When you choose to trust God completely, and appropriate His resources to meet your every need, you will begin to experience victory over your sinful nature, not because you will eliminate it entirely, but because you will be following the One who *can*.

Question to Consider

As believers, we frequently use phrases like
"use me Lord" or "your will be done in my life."
What do you think is the primary hindrance
to His response to these types of requests?

Chapter 6

Misdirected Affections:

The External Enemy

In the previous chapter, we briefly discussed the war that rages between the believer and the three spiritual enemies — the world, the flesh, and the devil — focusing mainly on the flesh. We now turn our attention to how the world influences all believers.

Some have used the phrase "worldly Christians" to describe people who profess to be believers but live like the world. But, as Billy Sunday aptly conveyed, a "worldly Christian" is a misnomer. He said, "To talk about a worldly Christian makes about as much sense as talking about a Heavenly Devil."[27]

This claim is supported by C.J. Mahaney, who stated, "The greatest challenge facing American evangelicals is not persecution from the world, but seduction by the world."[28] Further, George Gallup stated in an address before the national gathering of Southern Baptist leaders, "We find there is very little difference in ethical behavior between churchgoers and those who are not active religiously.... The levels of lying, cheating, and stealing are remarkably similar in both groups."[29]

Christians acting like non-Christians is not an exclusive characteristic of the modern Church. Throughout both his Gospel and his Epistles, the apostle John contrasts these antithetical groups using strong word imagery:

- Light verses darkness
- Love verses hate
- Children of God verses Children of the Devil
- Righteousness verses unrighteousness
- Obedience verses disobedience
- Love for God verses Love for the world

The Christian life is not a playground, but a battleground. You are hindered from walking on the narrow path by distractions vying for your attention and affection. The world can be one of the greatest caustic influences in the life of the new believer, and John was no stranger to this reality. In 1 John 2:15-17, he gives a warning against worldliness, highlights the wickedness of worldliness, and describes the worthlessness of worldliness.

Warning against Worldliness

John's readers are by no means to love the world. "Do not love the world or the things that belong to the world. If anyone loves the world, love for the Father is not in him" (1 John 2:15). These words represent a decisive command to his audience. John is not attempting to restrict their happiness. Rather, he attempts to promote it, stating that their affection is reserved for another — God. The world offers things that, from the outside, appeal to and entice the Christian with temporary pleasures. But, ultimately, they stand as boundaries between us and a relationship with God, the true joy of a Christian's existence. God creates hedges to protect us and to maintain fellowship with us.

The Greek word "kosmon," translated "world," occurs twenty-three times in 1 John, and can be translated to have three different meanings. The first is "planet." This rendering describes the natural world and can be found expressing such a meaning in 1 John 3:17. The second translation is "people." This description can be expressed in general terms, as in John 3:16, "For God loved the world [i.e., people]..." It is also used to describe people who are opposed to God and are in allegiance to Satan, as in 1 John 3:1: "The reason the world does not know us is that it didn't know Him." The final interpretation of "world" is "pattern" — the system of this present world with values and attitudes that are in opposition to God. Based on the context, John has the third interpretation in mind. Since we are talking about the pattern of the world, I have chosen to use the word "worldliness" for the sake of clarity.

So, what then is "worldliness?" It is the pursuit of pleasing and exalting oneself at the expense of abandoning God. It places man or self at the center of life rather than God. In his book, *Family Survival in the American Jungle*, Dave Roper comments:

> *Worldliness is not just about reading certain magazines of people who live hedonistic lives and spend too much money on themselves and secretly wanting to be like them. More importantly, worldliness is simply pride and selfishness in disguise. It's being resentful when someone snubs us or patronizes us or shows off. It means smarting under every slight, challenging every word spoken against us, cringing when another is preferred before us. Worldliness is harboring grudges, nursing grievances, and wallowing in self-pity. These are some of the ways in which we evidence a love for the world.*[30]

John continues by stating, "Do not love the world or the things that belong to the world. If anyone loves the world, love for the Father is not in him" (1 John 2:15). We have three options for interpreting the phrase "love of the Father." The first is to take the phrase to mean God's love for believers (1 John 4:9). Second, it can also be understood as referring to a believers' love for God (John 5:3). Third, it can be taken to refer to the love that comes from God and is expressed through believers to others (1 John 3:17, 4:7). In the present passage, the second option is arguably correct since love for the world is in opposition to love for God. This is further supported by the way John uses this phrase elsewhere: "For this is what love for God is: to keep His commands. Now His commands are not a burden." (1 John 5:3). Just like Jesus, John states that if you love God, you will keep His commandments.

Subsequently, "If you love the world," clarifies John, "love for God is not in you." He merely reiterates what Jesus claimed in the Gospels, "You cannot serve two masters. You will love one and hate the other. You cannot serve both God and the world" (Luke 16:30). The heart cannot embrace two opposing affections at the same time. You either love God or love the world. The choice is that simple.

Questions to Consider

How would you describe what the Bible calls "the world"? Why is the love for the things of the world in opposition to a love for God?

Wickedness of Worldliness

Following his warning against wickedness, John describes the negative influences of the world: "For everything that belongs to the world — the lust of the flesh, the lust of the eyes, and the pride in one's lifestyle — is not from the Father, but is from the world" (1 John 2:16). John breaks the world system into three elements: 1) the desires of the flesh, 2) the desires of life, and 3) the pride of life.

Desires of the Flesh

This Greek word translated "desire" is used sixteen times in the New Testament, only four of which use the word in a positive manner. Here are two examples of "desire" used in that way. Jesus said in Luke 22:15, "I have earnestly *desired* to eat the Passover with you" (emphasis added). Paul writes in Philippians 1:23, "I am hard pressed between the two. My *desire* is to depart and be with Christ, for that is far better" (emphasis added). In twelve instances, "desire" carries a negative connotation. The word can also be translated as "craving" or "lust."

The "desires of the flesh," like "the desires of the eyes" and "the pride of life," is a broad category that can take on numerous expressions. The problem is not that we crave things, but that we crave things too much. The flesh never has enough. The craving for clothes never ends. It starts as an interest and ends as an obsession. The craving for money starts as a desire and ends as a demand. The desire for recognition begins as flattery and ends as self-obsession, always desiring more and more acclaim.

Genevan pastor and theologian John Calvin rightly exclaimed, "Our hearts are perpetual factories of idols."[31] Humans are constantly manufacturing new idols to worship, attempting to fill the void meant to be satisfied by God. These desires are not bad in and of themselves, but when they dominate our lives, they are detrimental to our spiritual well-being.

Desires of the Eyes

The lusts of the eyes are those things that our eyes crave, which ultimately lead to coveting. It is the indulgence of glitter, glare, and glamor. The eyes are the windows to the soul. They act as gatekeepers to the outside world. Once an image is implanted in your mind, it is nearly impossible to remove. Like a stain on a dress, the pictures are permanently imbedded in your conscience mind. The answer to the following questions will help determine how you are doing in this area. What do you think about most of the time? Where does your mind wander when you have idle time?

Pride of Life or Possessions

Yusuf Ismail was Europe's heavyweight wrestling champ a little over two generations ago. His nickname was the "Terrible Turk" because of his massive size — he was around 350 pounds — and herculean strength. After he won the championship in Europe, he sailed to America to challenge the U. S. champion,

"Strangler Lewis," a much smaller man who weighed just over two hundred pounds, some one hundred and fifty pounds less than his European opponent.

Strangler Lewis, as his name suggests, was known for defeating his opponents by "choking them out." He would squeeze his opponents' necks until they passed out from lack of oxygen to the brain. Many an opponent had passed out in the ring as a result of the Strangler's technique. The problem Lewis discovered when it came to fighting the Terrible Turk was that the European giant didn't have a neck. His head seemed connected directly to his massive shoulders. In the ring, Strangler Lewis was unable to grasp hold of his opponent, so Yusuf hurled Lewis over onto the mat and pinned him for the win.

After winning the championship, the Terrible Turk requested that all of his $5,000 prize money be paid to him in gold. He wrapped the championship belt around his huge midsection, tucked the gold into his belt, and sailed on the next ship back to Europe. Halfway across the Atlantic, a storm struck the SS Bourgogne, and it began to sink. Yusuf was flung overboard with his gold belt still wrapped around his body. Refusing to relinquish his belt, the heavyweight champion struggled in the water because of the added weight. Like a millstone, he sunk to the bottom and was never seen again.[32]

You may be wondering, "Why didn't he take the belt off?" You may call him foolish or insane, but we are guilty-as-charged for the same shortcoming. We may have to loosen our grip on temporal objects in this world. When we let go of the things of this world, we begin to discern the difference between that which is temporal and that which is eternal, the things that matter in this life.

Who Owns Your Possessions?

Having possessions is, by itself, not a bad thing. It's when we find our identity in the things we have, or joy in the things we have acquired at the expense of God, that we have sinned. Truett Cathy, founder of Chick-fil-A, provides one of the greatest examples of how possessions can be used for the furtherance of the kingdom. His goal was to establish the most successful chicken restaurant on the planet in order to fund his pursuit to advance the kingdom of God. He parlayed a secular enterprise into a platform for spreading the gospel. Can you relate to this example? Is your goal to use what God gives you to make a spiritual impact in this world?

Imagine that I was hired to follow you for a week to determine whether or not you were a true follower of the Lord Jesus. At the end of the week, I am to present a full report of everything I observed. The report would include music playlists, purchases in stores and online, websites you frequented, every conversation you engaged in, every text message you have sent and received, all of your emails coming in and going out, every television show you viewed, and all of your thoughts, actions, and attitudes.

Would I be able to identify you as a believer? Could I determine the difference between you and an unbeliever by the music you listen to, the places you go, the people with whom you hang out, or the way you talk? Are you any different than your unbelieving neighbors, co-workers, family members, or friends? An even more poignant question to ask might be this: Can your children tell the difference? They see you every day. Better yet, can your family tell a difference? *Would a prosecuting attorney have enough evidence to convict you as a Christian?* Good works will not earn our salvation from God, but they will build the case of proof for our faith on the last day. Do you have a deep abiding love for God or an adulterous love affair with the world?

Question to Consider

*Why are believers so attracted
to the world's system?*

Worthlessness of Worldliness

Not only does Paul warn against the wickedness of worldliness, but he also describes the worthlessness of worldliness. Why would a believer invest their efforts in a world that, according to John, "with its lust is passing away"? (1 John 2:17). The word "passing" is in the present tense, indicating an ongoing process. In 1 Corinthians 7:31 Paul makes virtually the same point when he contends, "For the present form of this world is passing away." An investment in worldliness is worthless.

One of the most disheartening portions of the New Testament is the biography of Demas. As a close friend and traveling companion of Paul, he abandoned the security of his home to accompany Paul abroad throughout Asia Minor and the Balkan region. Throughout his ministry, he demonstrated substantial commitment to the work of the Lord. Paul mentions him in Philemon 23-24: "Epaphras, my fellow prisoner in Christ Jesus, greets you, and so do Mark, Aristarchus, Demas, and Luke, my coworkers." Think of the company of men by whom Demas was surrounded! Paul mentions him again in Colossians 4:14: "Luke, the dearly loved physician, and Demas greet you." We know that Paul possessed marginal tolerance for consumerism or casual Christianity from his response to Barnabas after the incident with John Mark (Acts 15:36-39). A longtime friendship with Barnabas was severed as a result of Mark's apparent cowardice on their missionary journey. Being a travel companion of Paul was a privilege; being mentioned in his letters is an incalculable honor.

The significance of his partnership with Paul is highlighted when you realize that Paul is writing these letters from prison. Initially, Demas is by his side, shouldering the burden by providing food, support, and encouragement. The fact that Paul sends greetings on behalf of Demas to Colossae and to Philemon's community demonstrates that the local body of believers knew him well. He probably stayed in their homes, shared meals with them, and exchanged testimonies of God's grace. But something happened along the way.

Paul, writing from a prison cell just moments before his death, pens his final letter to Timothy. In his closing remarks, he writes these sobering words, which were certainly filled with anguish and despair: "Demas has deserted me, because he loved this present world, and has gone to Thessalonica" (2 Timothy 4:10). Paul, two verses before, proclaimed, "I have fought the good fight, I have finished the race, I have kept the faith." Apparently, Demas had not.

We can sense the heartbreak Paul was experiencing. What a wasted life! His testimony was ruined. The name of Christ was dragged through the mud. Demas not only deserted Paul, his friend and mentor, but more importantly he deserted Jesus. How did it happen? Was it immediate? Probably not. Worldliness always creeps in subtly, with a compromise here and a compromise there. Destruction always starts with a slow fade. C. J. Mahaney is helpful once again:

> *So often we're ignorant of the signs, the symptoms of worldliness. People can be attending church, singing the songs, apparently listening to the sermons — no different on the outside than they've always been. But inside, that person is drifting. He sits in the church but is not excited to be there. She sings songs without affection. He listens to preaching without conviction. She hears but does not apply. It begins with a dull conscience and a listless soul. Sin does not grieve him like it once did. Passions for the Savior begin to cool. Affections grow dim. Excitement lessens for participating in the local church. Eagerness to evangelize starts to wane. Growth in godliness slows to a crawl.*[33]

The difference between a disciple and a drifter is unnoticeable. You may say, "We have been busy with sports and activities. Pastor, we are playing summer ball, and you know how busy summer ball can be. I have not been as faithful to the Lord as I need to be, but I'm fine. We'll be back to church soon." Or perhaps you are one to say, "I've just been so busy at work, and by the time I get home I'm spent. There is no time for fellowship with other believers, reading my Bible, or service to the Lord. I know I haven't spent time with anyone from church in a few months, but I'm good. I haven't left God or anything. I will get back on track in a few weeks."

Has there been a time where you were sold out to God? Was there a time when you were so passionate about the effects of the gospel in your life that you would tell everyone you came in contact with? Demas was once like that. But something happened. Has a love for the world choked out your love for Christ? Maybe it is due to

>   ... preoccupations with temporal things,
>   ... possessions,
>   ... popularity,
>   ... power,
>   ... position,
>   ... people-pleasing, or
>   ... pride.

Pilots tell me that to fly a plane a number of factors need to be taken into consideration. You must determine the distance, altitude, wind speed, and direction before traveling from point A to point B. For example, if you fly your aircraft in a certain direction without considering the wind direction and speed, you will be nudged off course throughout the journey. A half-degree difference may not seem like much at the start, but over a one hundred mile journey, you could find yourself as far as fifteen miles off course. The same goes for the Christian life. One compromise here or there might seem negligible, but over the course of a few months or a year, it can be tragic.

Questions to Consider

Which of these things, the desires of the flesh, desires of the eyes, or the pride of life/possessions, hinders you from pursuing God faithfully? What are some practical ways to avoid worldly attractions that easily misdirect your affection for God?

The Worth of an Eternal Investment

John begins with a warning against worldliness, but he ends with a promise: "And the world with its lust is passing away, but the one who does God's will remains forever" (1 John 2:17). "Abide" is another word for "remain" or "live forever." What a great promise for those who resist the lusts of the flesh, the lusts of the eyes, and the pride of possessions! Their satisfaction in God will remain forever. The pursuit of worldliness, on the other hand, is always a bottomless pit. Fortune and fame in the world always leaves you wanting more.

J.D. Rockefeller built Standard Oil (which would eventually become Exxon) into one of the most profitable companies in history. As a result, Rockefeller became the wealthiest man in the world. He was asked one time, "How much is enough money?" He replied, "Just a little bit more."[34] After Rockefeller died in 1937, someone asked, "How much money did he leave behind?" An executor for his estate replied, "All of it!"[35] Over my years as pastor, I have officiated many funerals, and have yet to see a U-Haul behind a hearse.

I think of people like Ernest Hemingway, Vincent van Gogh, Marilyn Monroe, Janis Joplin, John Belushi, Kurt Cobain, Chris Farley, Michael Jackson, Whitney Houston and many more, who, by the world's standards, had it all. While God is the only one who knew the state of their soul when they died, I do know they all died a premature death. They achieved the pinnacle of fame and fortune, yet privately they battled anxiety, depression, and loneliness. The words of Jesus provide a haunting reminder for us to keep our eyes on the eternal: "What does it benefit a man to gain the whole world yet lose his life?" (Mark 8.36).

Helen H. Lemmel was a gifted concert soloist, music teacher, and music critic. The inspiration for a hymn she wrote was a tract written by Lilias Trotter entitled, *The Heavenly Vision*. Trotter had a lucrative profession as an artist, but her other love was missions. After struggling in prayer for two years, Trotter realized that she must lay down her love of art to fix her eyes solely on Jesus and the mission field. She would serve Him for the next thirty-eight years as a missionary to the Muslims in Algeria, Africa. She once stated,

Never has it been so easy to live in half a dozen harmless worlds at once—art, music, social science, games, motoring, one's profession, and so on. And between them we run the risk of drifting about, the good hiding the best. It is easy to find out what our lives are focused on. Where do our thoughts settle when consciousness comes back in the morning? Where do they swing back, when the pressure is off during the day? Turn your soul's vision to Jesus, and look at Him, and a strange dimness will come over all that is apart from Him.[36]

These words inspired Helen Lemmel to pen the great hymn many of us know well:

Turn your eyes upon Jesus,

Look full in His wonderful face.

And the things of earth will grow strangely dim,

In the light of His glory and grace.[37]

These words are a mantra to live by. Believers must rehearse the gospel daily. Remind yourself that Jesus is the source of our delight and satisfaction for our souls. Remember, worldliness dulls our affection for Him and distracts us from an eternal perspective. Reconsider how you spend your money and your time. Differentiate the temporal from the eternal. You'll be eternally glad you did.

Chapter 7

Knowing is Half the Battle:

The Infernal Enemy

In the previous chapters, we discussed the war that rages between the believer and two of the spiritual enemies — the world and the flesh — that attack us. In chapter five we described how the flesh restrains one's response to God's work and reveals a heart alienated from God. In chapter six we examined Paul's warning against the wickedness and worthlessness of worldliness. In this chapter we will turn our attention to the attacks of Satan and his minions.

As Adolf Hitler's appetite for power grew, so did the boundaries of his empire. The Third Reich marched across the European landscape, seizing territory with limited resistance. In some cases, cities fell after such meager skirmishes that they barely warrant the title "battle." The German army, with its technologically advanced armament, stormed underdeveloped nations. Numerous opponents put up a futile effort to resist Hitler's aggression, some fighting with as little as spears and rocks. It was no contest. These nations were ill-equipped against the advancements of mid-Twentieth Century warfare.

The conflict between Satan and those who oppose him mirrors the state of the European front during the early years of

World War II. Many of Satan's targets are unprepared to wage spiritual battle, and some remain completely oblivious that a war is raging behind the scenes. These Christians make for easy prey. As believers, we must understand that we are in the midst of a great spiritual struggle. Further, we should be aware of Satan's tactics and the armaments available to us in God's arsenal. The Lord has not left us alone in the trenches. He has extended to us both defensive and offensive tactics for victory.

Perhaps the clearest account of spiritual warfare can be found in Ephesians 6:10-20. The apostle Paul not only affirms that war has been declared, he warns that we are a hopelessly undersupplied and underpowered soldier *if* we do not wield the weapons God has issued to us. This otherworldly struggle will not end until Christ's return. No temporary ceasefire or truce is on the horizon. Fasten your helmets, brothers and sisters, because we are at war! Paul describes spiritual warfare in this way:

> *For our battle is not against flesh and blood, but against the rulers, against the authorities, against the world powers of this darkness, against the spiritual forces of evil in the heavens. This is why you must take up the full armor of God, so that you may be able to resist in the evil day, and having prepared everything, to take your stand.* (Ephesians 6:12-13)

At the end of every *G.I. Joe* cartoon was a public service announcement that resounded with the exclamation: "Now you know, and knowing is half the battle!" The creators of the series wanted to teach children that in life, just as in battle, awareness and understanding of one's culture and surroundings is essential when devising a plan for success. Likewise, to live a *victorious* Christian life, you must know the spiritual landscape in which you reside. This entails recognizing who your adversary is in order to create a strategy of resistance. Allow me to begin by providing you with a profile of our nemesis before giving you God-empowered weapons to withstand his attacks.

Questions to Consider

*Before reading the above introduction,
were you aware that Christians were in a
spiritual battle against the forces of Satan?
If so, what do you know about it?*

Who is Our Enemy?

In the final chapters of this book the nature of our spiritual battle armor will be discussed in detail. Here, similar to a military general examining a scouting report of an enemy's forces before advancement, we will examine in detail the combat techniques of our adversary, Satan.

Origin of the Devil

"Satan" is the Hebrew word for "adversary." Seven Old Testament books and every New Testament writer refer to Satan. He is often called:

- *the devil* (Matthew 4:1, 13:39, 25:41; Revelation 12:9, 20:2),
- *the serpent* (2 Corinthians 11:3; Revelation 12:9, 20:2 [cf. Genesis 3:1, 14]),
- *Beelzebub* (Matthew 10:25, 12:24, 27; Luke 11:15),
- *the ruler of this world* (John 12:31, 14:30, 16:11),
- *the evil one* (Matthew 13:9; 1 John 2:13),
- *the dragon* (Revelation 12:9).

Satan, like the rest of the demons, was a once-good angel, but as a consequence of sin, his right to serve God was permanently revoked. He is a created being who lacks a physical body; that is, he is a spirit characterized by high intellect, deep emotions, and strong will.

Satan is not a red-costumed man with a pointed tail and pitchfork, as depicted in the movies. At one time he was one of the most beautiful creatures in heaven. God, in Ezekiel 28, speaks to Satan, who stands behind the king of Tyre:

> *You were the seal of perfection, full of wisdom and perfect in beauty. You were in Eden, the garden of God. Every kind of precious stone covered you: carnelian, topaz, and diamond, beryl, onyx, and jasper, sapphire, turquoise and emerald. Your mountings and settings were crafted in gold; they were prepared on the day you were created.* (Ezekiel 28:12-13; 2 Corinthians 11:14)

Due to pride in his beauty (Ezekiel 28:17) and aspirations for God-like glory and authority, Satan was cast down from heaven by God. Isaiah 14 describes his fall:

> *Shining morning star, how you have fallen from the heavens! You destroyer of nations, you have been cut down to the ground. You said to yourself: "I will ascend to the heavens; I will set up my throne above the stars of God. I will sit on the mount of the gods' assembly, in the remotest parts of the North. I will ascend above the highest clouds; I will make myself like the Most High." But you will be brought down to Sheol into the deepest regions of the Pit.* (Isaiah 14:12-15)

The term "stars," in verses 12 and 13, is symbolic of angels elsewhere (Job 38:6, 7; Revelation 12:4). The five "I will" statements of verses 13 and 14 are literally true of Satan and metaphorically true of Babylon's citizens, to whom Isaiah is speaking in this passage:

- I will ascend to heaven above the stars of God;
- I will set my throne on high;

- I will sit on the mount of assembly in the far reaches of the north;
- I will ascend above the heights of the clouds;
- I will make myself like the Most High.

According to 1 Timothy 3:6, humans can exhibit similar behavior, as is seen most clearly in the story of Adam and Eve. Satan made his first appearance in human history in the Garden of Eden where he comes in the form of a serpent to tempt Eve (Genesis 3). Satan comes as a creature of the field, which was said to be under both divine and human authority (Genesis 1:26). He tempts Eve to sin by disobeying God's command not to eat of the tree of the knowledge of good and evil. He insisted that by eating the fruit, Eve and Adam would become like God, knowing good and evil.

Subsequently, Eve falls headlong into Satan's trap and, in her footsteps, so too does Adam. As a result, the entire human race has been plagued with death and hardship from that original sin (Romans 5:12-21). Adam and Eve, therefore, were banished from the Garden for the same type of sin for which Satan was cast out of heaven — the sin of desiring and striving to esteem one's self as equal to or higher than God.

Hence, Satan is ultimately a self-possessed liar who actively leads others into the same sins for which he has been convicted. It is his goal not to be the only one on the proverbial sinking ship. His desire is for the rest of creation to follow in his footsteps.

Questions to Consider

*Do you know anyone who is openly and
unrepentantly prideful, untruthful, or corrupt?
Are these traits that exemplify Christ or the devil?*

The Current Activity of the Devil

Before outlining the current activity of Satan, I must issue a disclaimer: Satan's power is limited by God's control over him. In Job, Satan could only do what God gave him permission to do. Jude 6 supports this supposition by stating, "He has kept, with eternal chains in darkness for the judgment of the great day, the angels who did not keep their own position but deserted their proper dwelling." Although Satan was the originator of sin, he can go no further with his schemes than God allows. He is, after all, a very powerful, but finite, creation of the Almighty.

Klyne Snodgrass' comment concerning the works of Satan captures the thrust of his mission: "Mention of the 'schemes' of the devil reminds us of the trickery and subterfuge by which evil and temptation present themselves in our lives. Evil rarely looks evil until it accomplishes its goal; it gains entrance by appearing attractive, desirable, and perfectly legitimate. It is a baited and camouflaged trap."[38] Satan seeks to oppose God's plan by promoting evil in every way possible both through *indirect activity* and *direct activity*.

Indirect Activity

The devil works indirectly through both the world and human flesh. Understand that the world, the flesh, and the devil are not three unrelated enemies of the Christian. Each work is a concerted effort to kill, steal, and destroy. Norm Geisler provides a helpful chart to demonstrate this alliance:

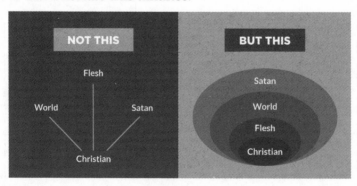

Figure 2[39]

As we can see, Satan works through the corrupt world system and the flesh to exploit the sinful nature that is at war within us. This axis of evil is straightforwardly opposed to the allied forces of Christians, the angels, and the Trinity.

Direct Activity

Since the devil is not omnipresent, he is restricted to being at one place at one time (Job 1:6-7; 1 Peter 5:8). You may have spoken the Flip Wilson line, "the devil made me do it." However, the chance he will attack you or me himself is highly improbable. Nevertheless, we shouldn't relax our guard or turn a blind eye to his attacks. First, Satan has demonic associates that work on his behalf to corrupt humanity. Second, those who are leaders of Christian communities are more susceptible to being attacked by Satan himself. The enemy and his demons attack through:

- False philosophies (Colossians 2:8),
- False religions (1 Corinthians 10:20),
- False teachers (2 Corinthians 11:14-15),
- False doctrine (1 John 2:18), and
- False morals (2 Thessalonians 2:7-12).

Satan tempts believers to exhibit anger (Ephesians 4:26-27), pride (1 Timothy 3:6), worldliness (1 John 2:18), untruthfulness (Acts 5:3), and immorality (1 Corinthians 4:4). Not only does he prey on Christians, he perpetually blinds unbelievers in their depraved condition (2 Corinthians 4:4). His attacks are always subtle and rarely seen. Since the demons are students of human actions, habits, and attitudes, and have been for millennia, the temptations are tailor-made for every person. C.S. Lewis wrote in his book *The Screwtape Letters*:

There is a legend about Satan and his imps planning their strategy for attacking the world that's hearing the message of salvation. One of the demons says, 'I've got the plan, master. When I get on earth and take charge of people's thinking, I'll tell them there's no heaven.'

The devil responds, 'Ah, they'll never believe that. This Book of Truth is full of messages about the hope of heaven through sins forgiven. They won't believe that. They know there's a glory yet future.' On the other side of the room another says, 'I've got a plan. I'll tell 'em there's no hell.' 'No good,' he says, 'Jesus, while He was on earth, talked more of hell than of heaven. They know in their hearts that their wrong will have to be taken care of in some way. They deserve nothing more than hell.' And one brilliant little imp in the back stood up and said, 'Then I know the answer. I'll just tell them there's no hurry.' And he's the one Satan chose.[40]

If the attacks against Christians are custom-made, the question arises: Can the devil or demons, on a supernatural level, understand one's thoughts and interact directly with a person's mind? As with any complex doctrine, scholars disagree. There are at least two opposing beliefs. Some believe that Satan has the ability to know and tempt the minds of his Christian victims. Alternatively, there are those who suggest Satan has no such powers; rather, his temptations come only through external stimuli. So which one is it? Scripture does not provide a detailed outline into how he carries out his plans. Nonetheless, based upon what we do know of Satan and God, we can make certain logical deductions.

From biblical accounts of demon-human interactions, Satan and his fallen associates have the ability to interrupt and manipulate the physical and mental activities of human beings. To do so, Satan and demons must "possess" a person — that is, enter into the victim's mind, heart, or both. The Holy Spirit is stronger than any fallen angel, including Satan. Therefore, since Christians are already possessed by the Spirit of God, Satan and his demons are powerless to supplant the Spirit in order to possess a believer. Hence, Christians are protected from possession through the inner-presence of the Holy Spirit.

The devil and his demons are unable to discern the future (Mark 13:32), nor can they read the thoughts of Christians. Still, Satan can tempt us through external means. He works through the world's system and appeals to our flesh. According to James 1:14-15, this form of temptation is extremely dangerous: "But each person is tempted when he is drawn away and enticed by his own evil desires. Then after desire has conceived, it gives birth to sin, and when sin is fully grown, it gives birth to death."

My point is worth repeating. Believers cannot be *possessed* or *controlled* by Satan. He personally cannot get into a believer's head. Nevertheless, this does not mean that he cannot *oppress* us. Through the world's influences he can tempt us to conform ourselves to his image rather than the image of Christ. Satan is a finite, created creature like us. He is smart, but he is not omniscient. He is strong, but he is not omnipotent. He is fast, but he is not omnipresent.

Questions to Consider

Is there anyone or anything in this world that tempts you to sin? Would God be honored if you stopped interacting with that person or thing?

Minions in His Military

According to Paul, Satan does not work alone: "For our battle is not against flesh and blood, but against the rulers, against the authorities, against the world powers of this darkness, against the spiritual forces of evil in the heavens" (Ephesians 6:12). Several important observations about the character of Satan's assault arise in this text. First, by distinguishing "flesh and blood" from "cosmic powers," Paul asserts that people are not our enemy. On the contrary, unbelievers are enslaved by the enemy.

Consider what Paul says elsewhere in 2 Timothy 2:25-26: "Perhaps God will grant them repentance leading them to the knowledge of the truth. Then they may come to their senses and escape the Devil's trap, having been captured by him to do his will." Our enemies' abode is the supernatural realm. Their mission on earth is to be a caustic influence; they plan to engulf humans into the bondage of sin and death. So we should refrain from attacking humans directly and maliciously. As believers, we should approach outsiders with graciousness and compassion, with prayer for their well-being and expedient release from Satan's grasp.

Second, Paul is not diagraming a hierarchical structure of the demonic realm where one evil force reports to another cosmic power. He offers no flowchart of corruption. Ephesus, we must remember, was a cesspool of spiritual wickedness. Magical practices mixed with astrological beliefs were the norm of the culture. The cult of Artemis had many converts, along with the pagan Phrygian mystery religions. In a place where sorcery and magic were mainstays, Paul pens these words to celebrate the supremacy of Christ over every evil ruler, power, authority, and force that exists or are imagined to exist. Many of the believers in the Ephesian church hearing this letter came out of such mystical paganism. These words were comforting to them, though they may be confusing to us. We must constantly remind ourselves that our struggle is with the supernatural. Paul says, *"We do not wrestle against flesh and blood"* (Ephesians 6:12). Our combat is not against physical and temporal people. What we war against is not of the natural world, but the otherworldly.

Third, it is important to remember that our struggle is personal. The word "wrestle" or "struggle" indicates a hand-to-hand fight. The idea behind the word is of two opponents swaying back and forth while locked in close combat. An exchange of arrows or artillery is not envisioned here. Fighting with the demonic is CQB — "Close Quarters Battle."

Fourth, we should recall that without Christ and His weapons of war, our struggle is an exercise in futility. As mentioned earlier, in our own strength we are incapable of victory. Humans engaged in a superhuman battle will not prevail with mainstream tactics. John Calvin writes, "He [Paul] means that our difficulties are far greater than if we had to fight against men. Where we resist human strength, sword is opposed to sword, man contends with man, force is met by force, and skill by skill; but here the case is very different, for our enemies are such as no human power can withstand."[41]

It would be much easier to fight an enemy whose attacks were out in the open and simple to identify. But, unfortunately, they are not. Satanic and demonic oppression is subtle, hidden, and extremely effective. One well-placed, well-hidden sniper can hold off an entire platoon for the sheer fact that he or she cannot be readily found and eliminated. So, too, can the strategically administered and understated attacks of our supernatural opponents hinder the advancement of the kingdom if its citizens cannot and do not defend themselves against such assaults.

Once again, C.S. Lewis' book, *The Screwtape Letters*, paints a picture of the spiritual realm with an older demon counseling a younger demon. At one point in the book, he declares:

> *You will say that these are very small sins, and doubtless, like all young tempters, you are anxious to be able to report spectacular wickedness. But do remember, the only thing that matters is the extent to which you separate the man from the Enemy [God]. It does not matter how small the sins are, provided that their cumulative effect is to keep the man away from the Light. Murder is no better than cards if cards can do the trick. Indeed the safest road to Hell is the gradual one, the gentle slope, soft underfoot, without sudden turnings, without milestones, without signposts.*[42]

Questions to Consider

Christians are known for openly protesting and slandering homosexuals, abortionists, and corrupt politicians. But based on what we have learned from Ephesians 6:12, is this the proper Christian response? How, then, should we respond to the world's wickedness?

The Enemy Has Been Defeated

In the fall of 1944, Nazi Germany had been nearly destroyed from the bombings of allied troops. Hitler would surely never rise to power again. People celebrated the upcoming victory over Germany across Europe and Great Britain. The problem was that the German soldiers didn't get the message that the war was over.

Until his final days on earth, Hitler was scheming and planning a new attack. He was producing weapons and ammunition from underground factories. German boys and men were being enlisted and trained for battle. While the allied forces celebrated, Hitler was conspiring. He established a plan to disrupt communication between the British in the North and the Americans in the South by occupying the middle ground. On what was called the Battle of the Bulge, one million men fought across an eighty-five mile front for over a month. Thousands of men lost their lives in this bloody battle. [43] His advancement sealed the fate of his men and the end of the war. He didn't realize he was defeated before the battle began.

Similarly, Satan has been utterly defeated through the cross of Christ. What appeared to be Satan's greatest victory was actually his ultimate defeat. Although Christ was completely and utterly humiliated through His trial, crucifixion and death, the cross was the means by which Christ debased Satan and disarmed death (Colossians 2:15). Even though Christ is the victor, the war is not over. Satan continues to lead a covert battle of deception. The devil seeks to convince us that he still has power over our lives and that he has the right to take back territory Christ has won. But don't be afraid, for the "One who is in you is greater than the one who is in the world" (1 John 4:4).

Question to Consider

Do you have a greater fear of Satan, who has been tried, convicted, and awaits punishment, or Christ in heaven, who is already victorious through the cross?

Stand in His Strength

Before we send the cavalry in the direction of the enemy, we should note that Paul instructs the believers to "be strong in the Lord and in the strength of his might" (Ephesians 6:10 [ESV]). The imperative "be strong," can be translated, "be strengthened" or "made strong." One would expect the verb to be an active verb, implying an action performed by the readers; however, the verb is passive, indicating an action *received* by God, not *achieved* by man. God is the author and initiator of the action. Paul uses the same verb in Ephesians 3:14-16: "For this reason I kneel before the Father from whom every family in heaven and on earth is named. I pray that He may grant you, according to the riches of His glory, to be strengthened with power in the inner man through His Spirit."

Because of the death, burial, and resurrection of Christ and the bestowal of the Holy Spirit, Christians no longer live under Satan's tyranny. At one time we were spiritually dead, "carrying out the inclinations of our flesh and thoughts, and we were by nature children under wrath as the others were also" (Ephesians 2:3). But now, because of God's love for us and for the sake of His glory, we have been made "alive together with Christ. . . and [God has] raised us up together, and made us sit together in the heavenly places in Christ Jesus" (Ephesians 2:5-6; NKJV). Therefore, due to our new standing before God and position in Christ, Christians are strengthened in Him through "the riches of his glory" (Ephesians 3:16).

The only way we can overcome the devil is through the strength of the Lord. Any Christian standing in his or her own power against the devil and his host of unseen cohorts is destined for failure. If Christians are prone to lose this war against Satan, how much more will unbelievers? There is no hope for unbelievers to resist him apart from the regeneration and subsequent empowerment of the Spirit. Their only hope is a right relationship with Jesus.

We have an active opponent with the ferocious hunting instincts of a lion (1 Peter 5:8) who can only be defeated through the power of the cross and the ongoing work of the Holy Spirit. Victory is realized when we appropriate the power entrusted to us by God through His Spirit.

So now that we know our enemy, we need a battle plan to withstand the enemy. We must reinforce our positions. If you are employing tactics in your own strength, you will not win, for "the weapons of our warfare are not worldly, but are powerful through God for the demolition of strongholds" (2 Corinthians 10:4).

Question to Consider

What does Paul mean by "the weapons of our warfare are not worldly" in 2 Corinthians 10:4?

Chapter 8
Triumphing Over Temptation:

The Internal Enemy

An unfortunate number of young believers embark on the Christian journey with unrealistic expectations of never struggling with past sins that have wreaked havoc on their lives and relationships. Unfortunately, believers are not exempt from temptation. As we have already learned, the flesh, the world, and the devil stand as pervasive threats to the believer. As long as we are in these earthly bodies, plagued with our sinful nature, we will face temptation. The good news is that, as believers, we have access to supernatural resources to help us triumph over it. In this chapter, we will discuss the source and sequence of temptation before providing a framework for overcoming temptation.

In his first epistle to the Corinthians, Paul taught that all believers struggle with temptation (1 Corinthians 10:13). James affirmed this troubling fact stating that "each person is tempted" (James 1:14). Everyone, believer and non-believer alike, struggles with temptation. If you deny this unalterable fact, you're sinning right now by lying to yourself. While we all wrestle with temptation, however, different people are enticed by different sins (James 1:14). Hebrews 12:1 speaks of "the sin which so easily ensnares us" (NASB). The particular sin that most powerfully tempts me may differ from the sin that appeals most to you. Russell Moore elaborates on this:

> When I say that we share common temptations, don't get me wrong. I am not saying that we all experience this temptation in precisely the same way. Maybe you tear up when you think about the words you screamed at your kids this morning. Maybe you've deleted the history cache on your computer this week, promising yourself you'll never access those images again. Maybe you carry that empty snack bag with you in your purse to throw away later so the people in your office won't see it in the wastebasket. Maybe the prescription drugs in your desk drawer are the only things keeping you sane, but you fear they're making you crazy. Maybe you just can't stop thinking about the smell of your coworker's hair or the clink of the whiskey glass at the table nearby.[44]

The scope of sin is immeasurable, but the promise of its presence is universal.

Discipleship Journal asked its readers to rank the areas of temptation they struggle with the most. The results came back in this order:

1. Materialism
2. Pride
3. Self-centeredness
4. Laziness
5. Anger/bitterness and sexual lust (tied for fifth place)[45]

It is important for believers to identify sins that are the most powerfully appealing to them. Do you crave possessions? Do you thirst for alcohol or drugs? Do you desperately seek the latest morsel of juicy gossip? Do you wrestle with lying, disrespect for authorities, uncontrolled anger, or lustful thoughts? Do you promote yourself at the expense of others? Are you lazy? Self-centered? Abusive? Do you over-eat? Do you cheat on your taxes?

Every human is confronted with temptation on a daily, if not hourly, basis. How are we to deal with these temptations when they arise? Before we can triumph over temptation, we must first understand it.

Point to Ponder

*Take a moment to identify and rank those things
in your life that you clearly recognize as sins.*

Where Does Temptation Come From?

Temptation is not from God. "No one undergoing a trial should say, 'I am being tempted by God.' For God is not tempted by evil, and He Himself doesn't tempt anyone" (James 1:13). Temptation is the natural consequence of our depraved nature. God is not responsible for this urge, and therefore cannot be blamed for our failures. This is why James unflinchingly exclaimed, "Let no one say." His language is emphatic. Bluntly stated, James says, "Don't even think of blaming God when you are tempted! God is not responsible for your temptation!"

Why was James so forceful with this matter? We are not to accuse God of leading us into unrighteousness because it is not within His character to do so. That is, God does not tempt us because evil is in stark conflict with His nature. While He often brings forth good from the evil that men do (as He did in Joseph's life in Genesis 50:20), God never incites people to sin in order that He may work good through it. Whenever we suggest that God is somehow involved in people sinning, we blatantly — and even blasphemously — accuse God of evil. Solomon stated the condemning truth about this tendency of our sinful nature: "A man's own foolishness leads him astray, yet his heart rages against the Lord" (Proverbs 19:3). Philo of Alexandria, a philosopher who lived during the time of Christ, restated this truth, saying, "When the mind has sinned and removed itself far from virtue, it lays the blame on divine causes."[46] We must staunchly reject the false notion that temptation is somehow God's fault.

Some may question this truth by citing the words of Jesus as He instructed His disciples in the Lord's Prayer: "And lead us not into temptation" (Matthew 6:12). Does this imply that God normally leads us into temptation and that we must appeal to Him not to do so? Absolutely not! Jesus is simply teaching us to ask the Father to prevent Satan from placing stumbling blocks in our path (Matthew 6:13). We should pray for God to redirect our plans and our steps to steer us clear from temptations snare. However, should God permit us to face temptation, we ask, "deliver us from evil," knowing that He always provides a way of escape (1 Corinthians 10:13).

James and Jesus did not suggest that God never allows us to face temptation. Furthermore, they are not ignoring the fact that God tests His people, just as He tested Abraham and Job. He may permit us to be placed in situations where we may be tempted, but God is not the source of our temptation. On the contrary, He is our rescuer and redeemer from it.

Is It Satan's Fault?

Where, then, does temptation come from? Some might be inclined to trace the origins of temptation to Satan. Flip Wilson, as mentioned earlier, was a popular American comedian in the 1960's and 1970's. His most-loved routine revolved around a character who frequently justified her misbehavior by stating, "The devil made me do it!" This line became a national catchphrase, even sparking a line of tee shirts. However, James doesn't even mention Satan in his lesson on temptation. James surely knew that Satan constantly tempts believers to sin, but he also knew the root of sin lies *within* us. "But each person is tempted when he is drawn away and enticed by his own evil desires. Then after desire has conceived, it gives birth to sin, and when sin is fully grown, it gives birth to death" (James 1:14-15). Temptation stems from our own evil desires.

Paul echoes this same truth in Romans 5:12, stating: "Therefore, just as sin entered the world through one man, and death through sin, in this way death spread to all men, because all sinned." Because of Adam, we all have an inherent sinful nature.

Dietrich Bonhoeffer, the German theologian executed by the Nazis for taking a stand against Hitler's regime, wrote:

In our members there is a slumbering inclination towards desire, which is both sudden and fierce. With irresistible power, desire seizes mastery over the flesh. All at once a secret, smoldering fire is kindled. The flesh burns and is in flames. It makes no difference whether it is sexual desire, or ambition, or vanity, or desire for revenge, love of fame and power, or greed for money, or, finally, that strange desire for the beauty of the world, of nature. Joy in God is in course of being extinguished in us and we seek all our joy in the creature. At this moment God is quite unreal to us, he loses all reality, and only desire for the creature is real; the only reality is the devil. Satan does not here fill us with hatred of God, but with forgetfulness of God. It is that everything within me rises up against the Word of God.[47]

In summary, **Bonhoeffer explains that the farther we get from God, the less real He appears to us.** The more our actions and thoughts reveal someone unworthy of God's presence, the easier it becomes to succumb to the temptations of the flesh. The farther we stray from God, the harder it seems to get *back* to Him or to re-energize desires for the things of God, even though He hasn't departed from us. The issue is not God's, but ours. Sometimes we simply need a wake-up call to realize the depth of our sinfulness.

As sinners incrementally separated from the will of God, we resist the truth about our sinfulness. Therefore, when we are tempted, we search for someone else to blame. Being consumed with lust, covetousness, anger, or any sin, we tend to point our finger at God, Satan, or other people who we think have failed us. But James explicitly states that we ourselves are to blame.

We sin because our hearts are corrupt and are sinners who love to sin. The evil one schemes against us, as we discussed above, but he cannot force us to sin. Immorality, lust, greed, anger, and lying all originate within us. The desire to sin is there. The enemy merely arranges circumstances to provoke that desire. By placing the blame on the enemy, we attribute to him more power than he actually possesses. Even though the devil *can* tempt us just as he tempted Eve in the Garden, he is never held accountable for our sin. We are responsible for our own actions.

Questions to Consider

When you look over the list you made earlier, why do you think there is such a desire to see God as failing you or the devil as forcing you? Can you trace your own steps and see how you have become ensnared in some of these sins?

The Sequence of Sinfulness

Having clearly identified the source of temptation, James continues describing the sequence of temptation: "But each person is tempted when he is drawn away and enticed by his own evil desires" (James 1:14). The sneakiest aspect of sin is that it does not disguise itself in slimy clothes and slither its way into your life accompanied by a herald announcing its arrival. It will creep slowly and softly into a crevice and make its root there while it grows into something enormous. Temptation follows a pattern, and once we recognize it, we can begin to snip it where it roots.

The First Step: Temptation Begins with Deception

The first step in temptation is being "lured," "dragged away" as the NIV says, and "enticed" by our sinful desires. The term "lured" is a hunting term referring to baiting a trap in order to catch an unsuspecting animal. When the hungry creature is drawn to the bait and advances toward it, it finds itself unable to retreat. The word "enticed" is a fishing term which speaks of using bait to bring a fish out of hiding so that it might be hooked. You bait a hook with a juicy worm for two purposes: first, to *entice* the fish and, second, to *hide* the hook. To lure a fish from its safe hiding place, a fisherman must cast a lure that the fish cannot resist. Once the fish is intrigued, *all it sees is the attractiveness of the bait*. Desperately desiring the bait, the fish is oblivious to the hook. Whether "lured" or "enticed," the purpose of the bait is to deceive the prey in order to capture and kill it.

In the same way, we are enticed by sin, and when our sinful passions are excited, we are blind to its consequences. The fish does not see the hook, and neither do we. *But the hook is always there*. We are simply deceived into believing that it is not. The consequences of sin are real and they are deadly, but the shroud of our sinful desires cause us to ignore them. If we were to clearly see and understand the painful aftermath of our sin, we would doubtlessly choose a different path.

Tired of girls smearing lipstick all over the bathroom mirrors, a middle school principal marched them into the bathroom, where the custodian was waiting. "All these lipstick marks are making the work of our custodian very difficult," she began. "I want you to see how much effort cleaning the mirrors requires." The custodian proceeded to take a long-handled brush, dip it into the toilet bowl, and then use it to clean the mirrors. Not surprisingly, the lipstick marks were never a problem again. No girl pressed her lips against the grimy glass again. If we could see the real filth involved when we sin, we wouldn't be nearly as attracted to it.

We must remember that under the right — or better said, wrong — circumstances, every one of us is subject to taking the bait. Have you ever heard someone critically respond to the heinous sins of another by claiming: "I would never do that?" But, apart from the grace of God, and left to your own devices, you are capable of doing everything you've said "I would never do!" Your temptations are specifically tailored to you and, believe me, you have all that you can bear. So don't point the finger at others, because what you are struggling with is more than you can handle by yourself.

I once counseled a college student who was eventually arrested for possessing child pornography. After tracking him for some time, the police arrived at his house to confiscate his computer which contained hundreds of obscene pictures of young boys and girls. Sharp, good-looking, and intelligent, he was the last person anyone would have suspected of such an atrocious act. How did he end up committing such a reprehensible sin? It all started with an inquisitive look at a Playboy magazine, which led to a curious search on the internet. As time went on, he progressively looked more frequently, until one day his uncontrolled desire evolved into an addiction. A simple lustful thought snowballed into his eventual arrest for his perverted use of innocent children. Needless to say, he must bear the reproach of his loathsome sin the rest of his life, and both he and his family have been emotionally destroyed.

Because it is such a pervasive problem in our churches and society, allow me to sidetrack for a moment to discuss the dangers of Internet pornography — the downward spiral of this sin affects many. Viewing pornography is undeniably appealing to some, like all sins that entice the flesh. The problem is that porn never satisfies a person because ones desire is for an object that cannot reciprocate emotion. The law of diminishing returns enters into the equation, meaning that what once stimulated you becomes stale, creating the need for stronger forms and greater frequency of pornography, as in the case of the young man above.

In the meantime, you have become addicted to pornography. A porn addiction is a form of idolatry because the images slowly consume your life, leading to a sexual obsession. You may find it difficult to focus on work or enjoy free time because of your appetite for it. You convince yourself "It is harmless!" but then you wonder why physical intimacy with a person of the opposite sex is difficult. Or you notice the attraction you once had for your spouse has waned. Ultimately, lasting relationships become impossible for those who muddle the act of sex with true intimacy by living in a fantasy world. Therefore, what seemed to be harmless fun is actually an acid that corrodes both your mind and your heart, destroying your relationships in the process. The sin-seeker is left wanting more. *Sin will always take your farther than you want to go, keep you there longer than you want to stay, and charge you more than you want to pay.*

The sin with which you struggle may not be anything mentioned in this book, but *no* sin is without consequence. If you do not deal with unconfessed sin immediately, it will destroy your life and cause unnecessary pain to those around you. We should never succumb to the temptation of short-term sinful pleasure at the expense of a lifetime of satisfaction in Christ.

The writer of Hebrews recalls the story of Moses to demonstrate the value of our satisfaction in Christ: "By faith Moses, when he had grown up, refused to be called the son of Pharaoh's daughter and chose to suffer with the people of God rather than to enjoy the short-lived pleasure of sin. *For he considered the reproach because of the Messiah to be greater wealth than the treasures of Egypt, since his attention was on the reward*" (Hebrews 11:24-26; emphasis added).

Remember, the bait is undeniably attractive, but it conceals a deadly trap. *We must look for the hook.*

The Second Step: Temptation Results in Disobedience

After being "lured" and "enticed," the second step in the sequence of temptation is disobedience. Be careful not to allow sin to be a lofty, heady, theoretical concept. What sin is, by definition, is missing the standard that God has set for us. The first sin ever committed in the garden is a perfect example for us to consider.

God charged Adam and Eve with the enormous task of maintaining the garden around them. They were to tend to the animals, cultivate the plants, commune with God, and, as we know, avoid eating of the tree in the middle of the garden. God set parameters around them for their protection. He gave them instructions to follow and commandments to heed. When temptation approached Eve, it arrived in the form of something she was familiar with — one of the creatures she was charged with caring for.

The moment Eve took a bite of the fruit that God had forbidden, her eyes were opened just as the serpent had promised. Her insubordination released the floodgates for a life of disobedience to God. Once we supplant our own desire in the place of God's, we instantly miss the mark of what God demands. Temptation creeps in, causing us to disobey God's standard of perfection.

Point to Ponder

A popular modern worldview is that "sin" is an archaic religious term, and that people are primarily good but just make poor decisions sometimes. Why do you think this viewpoint is so attractive?

The Final Step: Temptation Ends in Death

The final step in the sequence of temptation is death: "Then after desire has conceived, it gives birth to sin, and when sin is fully grown, it gives birth to death" (James 1:15). Even though sinning may begin with a period of pleasure, it will eventually end in death — death to your relationships, death to your career, death to your marriage, death to your future, and possibly death to your earthly life. While all sin does not always result in premature physical death for the believer, it can certainly lead to it. (John spoke of sin that leads to death in 1 John 5:16-17.) James concluded his epistle with instructions for helping a wayward believer find his or her way back to the path of righteousness, thereby rescuing such a one from premature death: "My brothers, if any among you strays from the truth, and someone turns him back, let him know that whoever turns a sinner from the error of his way will save his life from death and cover a multitude of sins" (James 5:19-20).

Nowhere in the Bible is the power of temptation and the tragic consequences of sin more vividly illustrated than in the account of David's atrocious sin with Bathsheba (2 Samuel 11). One night David walked out onto his balcony and saw beautiful Bathsheba bathing in the distance. His lustful heart desired her, so he inquired about her, sent for her, slept with her, and impregnated her. Then, he tried to cover his sin by arranging the death of her husband, Uriah, who was one of David's mightiest and most loyal warriors.

Bathsheba is not without blame either! She was the wife of a man who had been at war for a long time. She understood that her roof was visible from the palace and that her nakedness would attract the attention of the handsome king. So she exposed her nakedness in the sight of others, accepted David's call to visit at the palace, and consented to the affair he initiated. Nowhere in the account of David and Bathsheba is there an implication of rape or that David's advances were unwanted. She was just as guilty as David. Their shared guilt can be seen also in the shared consequence of their sin — the death of their son. The failure of David painfully reminds us that no one is immune to sin. If David, the blessed king of Israel, the man after God's own heart, could fall so quickly, so can we.

The good news is that temptation can be resisted. God has given us a specific promise about temptation: "No temptation has overtaken you except what is common to humanity. God is faithful, and He will not allow you to be tempted beyond what you are able, but with the temptation He will also provide a way of escape so that you are able to bear it" (1 Corinthians 10:13). We can overcome temptation. God has promised to always offer us a way to escape. You must search for that path and become familiar with it *before* temptation strikes. You cannot wait until you are in front of your computer screen to start dealing with the temptation of pornography. You cannot wait until you are seated on the bar stool to start dealing with your struggle with alcohol. You cannot wait until you are yelling at your kids to deal with the problem of anger. You must begin where the sequence starts — with your desires.

How Can I Triumph over Temptation?

James does not leave his readers without a method for overcoming temptation: "By His own choice, He gave us a new birth by the message of truth so that we would be the firstfruits of His creatures" (James 1:18). First, we must saturate ourselves with God's Word in our battle against temptation. It is our most powerful weapon (Ephesians 6:17; Hebrews 4:12). By His Word, God created the world. By His Word, He spoke through the prophets. By His Word, we are saved, and by His Word, our lives are sustained. The Sword of the Spirit — God's inspired, infallible Word — secures victory over temptation. The psalmist testified: "How can a young man keep his way pure? By keeping Your word. I have sought You with all my heart; don't let me wander from Your commands. I have treasured Your word in my heart so that I may not sin against You" (Psalm 119:9-11).

What would happen in your life if you stored up God's Word in your heart? What kind of effect would that have on the sin gripping you? Where would the roots of sin have to rest if your life were filled with the Word of God? In *Growing Up: How to Be a Disciple Who Makes Disciples,* I presented some steps that will help with memorizing and meditating on God's Word:

Picture It – What does this spiritual truth look like? Visualize what the text is saying in your mind. Picture it as a reality in your life.

Ponder It – To use an old expression, mull it over. Think on it. Repeat it over and over to yourself. What does this text mean?

What do the individual words mean? What is God trying to express?

Personalize It – What does it mean specifically in your life? What does this look like in your life? What actions are needed for the truth to become a reality?

Pray Over It – Ask God to bring this truth to life in your everyday experience. Ask Him to make the truth real, and to reveal how you should respond.[48]

Encountering temptation doesn't infer that you lack faith. Believers are tempted in spite of their faith because of the fallen world we live in. We can't always control the temptations that arise in our lives, but we can control how we respond to them. How are you responding to temptation? Are you standing firm in holiness or are you surrendering to the pressures of your fleshly desires? James offered a promise to those who persevere through trials and temptations: "A man who endures trials is blessed, because when he passes the test he will receive the crown of life that God has promised to those who love Him" (James 1:12).

Second, in overcoming temptation it is important to maintain your focus. If I were to instruct you, "Whatever you do, keep yourself from thinking about a pink elephant wearing a tutu on a balance beam," you'd have a difficult time focusing on anything *but* that funny looking elephant. In the same way, the more that we focus on ridding ourselves of temptation, the more temptation, in some form or fashion, stays on our minds.

Consider the story of Peter walking on the water in Matthew 14. Peter listened to the call of his Master, clambered over the side of the boat feet first into the crashing sea around him. His eyes were locked with Jesus' as his feet stood like they were supported by cement below. However, as soon as Peter looked away at the wind-battered boat and the rushing tide underneath his sandals, he began to sink. It wasn't until he averted his eyes from Christ's that he succumbed to the sea.

Resisting temptation is exactly the same way. In order to experience victory, we must keep our eyes focused on the Messiah. When our attention is placed on what we struggle with, often times the struggle will simply become greater; when our attention is on the One who has overcome all struggles, the struggle dissipates.

The ultimate goal of resisting temptation is not merely to defeat it; rather, the goal is to be conformed to the image of Christ. We can only conform to that which we are focusing on. When we lose battles with temptation after making its defeat our focus, we become angry, frustrated, and defeated. We begin to *fear* it, rather than *flee* it. Our sense of victory at defeating temptation is squashed by our constant need to look over our shoulders for when it rears again. But when our focus is on Jesus rather than on the temptation, the things of earth, as the great hymn "Turn Your Eyes Upon Jesus" says, grow strangely dim. We become free.

Miles Stanford, quoting Norman Douty in his book *The Green Letters*, illustrates this principle:

> *If I am to be like Him, then God in His grace must do it, and the sooner I come to recognize it the sooner I will be delivered from another form of bondage. Throw down every endeavor and say, I cannot do it, the more I try the farther I get from His likeness. What shall I do? Ah, the Holy Spirit says, You cannot do it; just withdraw; come out of it. You have been in the arena, you have been endeavoring, you are a failure, come out and sit down, and as you sit there behold Him, look at Him. Don't try to be like Him, just look at Him. Just be occupied with Him. Forget about trying to be like Him. Instead of letting that fill your mind and heart, let Him fill it. Just behold Him, look upon Him through the Word. Come to the Word for one purpose and that is to meet the Lord. Not to get your mind crammed full of things about the sacred Word, but come to it to meet the Lord. Make it to be a medium, not of Biblical scholarship, but of fellowship with Christ. Behold the Lord.[49]*

In conclusion, while it is true that believers are free in Christ, one should consider the following questions before entering into anything involving the body:

1.   Will this practice benefit my body or harm it?
2.   Will this practice control me?
3.   Will this practice support the truth that the body is "for the Lord" who created it and intended it to be used for His glory?
4.   Will this practice glorify God?

In the end, our decision comes down to what is temporary and what is eternal. Will you seek temporary satisfaction here on earth, or will you seek everlasting satisfaction from God?

Questions to Consider

Take a moment to consider what God has said in His Word. Rather than a comprehensive list of things to avoid or an outline of best practices, God lays all of the weight on memorizing His Word. If you want to stop sinning, memorize His Word (Psalm 119:11). Why do you think that one thing is so set apart as a tool for victory?

Chapter 9

Suit Up for Battle:

Spiritual Warfare I

Each Memorial Day in the United States, Americans celebrate the courage and commitment of the men and women who fought for our country. We express thanks for those who fought in World War I and World War II, as well as those who waged war in the Korea, Vietnam, Iraq, and Afghanistan. Each of these men and women was equipped for battle before they engaged in it. Before leaving for duty, they were outfitted with combat attire — a helmet and a firearm for defense and protection. Skillfully trained, these soldiers were ready for any wartime scenario. However, when their fight was over, though some of the principles they learned carried over, much of their battle training became obsolete.

The same cannot be said for believers. Like the men and women of the armed forces, we all are in a battle, but our adversary is not of this world and our fight does not end until death. He does not attack with conventional weapons or familiar tactics, and a ceasefire will never be experienced while we are still on earth. There is no truce with him or his cohorts. We will fight to the end of our physical lives. With this in mind, the firmly planted, secure believer must have a battle plan. The previous eight chapters have worked to establish a firm biblical foundation. Yet without an action plan the believer is left with only theoretical knowledge. But, as we said above, a change of mind should lead to a change of actions. For this reason, this chapter and the next will set forth a tangible battle strategy to ensure that you are well equipped to enter, and thrive, amidst spiritual warfare. In this chapter, we will discuss the proper attire for battle — the armor of God. In the next chapter, we will discuss perhaps the most powerful weapon a believer can bring into battle — prayer.

Suit Up For Battle

As we briefly discussed in Chapter 7, our enemy is not ultimately other people. Since we are *not* fighting against "flesh and blood" (Ephesians 6:12), conventional weapons and tactics will not suffice. Take a close look at Paul's words in Ephesians 6:13-17:

This is why you must take up the full armor of God, so that you may be able to resist in the evil day, and having prepared everything, to take your stand. Stand, therefore, with truth like a belt around your waist, righteousness like armor on your chest, and your feet sandaled with readiness for the gospel of peace. In every situation take the shield of faith, and with it you will be able to extinguish all the flaming arrows of the evil one. Take the helmet of salvation, and the sword of the Spirit, which is God's word.

His command is firm, "Do not allow the enemy to catch you off guard." In verse 13, two forms of the same verb appear: "withstand" and "stand." Additionally, Paul offers the second of three exhortations to "stand" (Ephesians 6:11, 13, 14), each implying the need for divine empowerment. Additionally, it confirms that the devil can be resisted since God has provided all the necessary resources for the battle.

Paul's reference to "the evil day," the time between the two comings of Christ, reminds us to be on guard at all times. Don't get lulled into a false sense of security thinking the battle is over. Believers are to do everything in their power to resist the devil and rely on the power of God. Klyne Snodgrass states in his commentary:

> *If you seek a religion to make you comfortable, despite all its focus on peace and benefit, Christianity is not it. This is no religion for the weak or the lazy. Passive Christians cannot do the will of God; the very label 'passive Christian' is an oxymoron. A battle is going on, and contrary to our deception, we do not live on neutral turf. We either live for God or against Him. The choices we make either reflect God's character or the character of sin.*[50]

While you can fall into sin, you will never fall into righteousness. We must take an active role in our Christian life by shoring ourselves with the armor of God.

Question to Consider

*What does taking an "active role"
in spiritual warfare look like?*

Fasten the Belt of Truth (Ephesians 6:14a)

The terms and significance of the armor are drawn from Isaiah 11. Paul uses vivid language to paint a description of the soldier. He could have communicated the same thing by saying, "Put on truth, righteousness, readiness, peace, faith, and salvation," but he appeals for human action. Before going into battle, the belt was fastened around the short tunic worn by the soldier. Subsequently, the soldiers' arms were braced for battle. When the sword was not in use it was attached to the belt by means of a sheath. Likewise, believers are to be strengthened by the truth of God's Word and live according to it.

Jesus depicted the devil as "a murderer from the beginning, and [one who] *has not stood in the truth*, because *there is no truth in him*. When he tells a lie, he speaks from his own nature, because he is a liar and the father of liars" (John 8:44; emphasis added). Since deceit is a characteristic of the enemy, Paul stresses that truthfulness should define believers. Chuck Colson illuminates how the enemy marginalizes truth:

> *In a culture infected with moral AIDS [AutoImmune Deficiency Syndrome], words lose all meaning; or, they are manipulated to obscure meaning. Thus taxes become "revenue assessment enhancements;" perversion is "gay;" murder of unborn children is "freedom of choice;" Marxism in the church is called "liberation theology." These are all good words (in the Nazi era "the final solution" had a nice ring to it also). And everyone just nods unquestioningly. But when words lose their meaning, it is nearly impossible for the Word of God to be received. If sin and repentance mean nothing, then God's grace is irrelevant. Our preaching falls on deaf ears. This moral deafness leads to disaster. The Scriptures tell us it was when people accepted King Ahab's gross evils as "trivial" that fearsome judgment befell ancient Israel.*[51]

A believer must recognize sin for what it is and that no sin is above another. Each transgression is equally loathed by a holy God. The more tainted we allow truth to become, the more enticing candy-coated sin can seem.

Wear the Breastplate of Righteousness

The breastplate was a metal or layered-leather cover that protected the heart, chest, neck, and abdomen from attack. Two parts comprised this piece, one concealing the front of the body and another guarding the back of the body. Paul derives this imagery from Isaiah 59:17: "He put on righteousness as a breastplate." In the context of Isaiah, God suits up in preparation for the impending judgement. In Ephesians 6, however, the believer's actions should reflect God's righteous character.

We cannot generate a righteous lifestyle on our own, for "there is no one righteous, not even one" (Romans 3:10; Isaiah 64:4). But, as mentioned above, we can reflect God's righteousness through the inner-working of the Spirit. This is the lifestyle to which we have been called (Ephesians 4:1), not a lifestyle of worldliness. The enemy gains a foothold when the words of our lips contradict with the walk of our lives. However, when our righteousness in conduct is present, we have a defensive measure against the attacks of our adversary.

Several years ago, one of the leading golfers on the professional tour was invited to play in a foursome with Gerald Ford — the then President of the United States — Jack Nicklaus, and Billy Graham. The golfer was excited to play with President Ford and Graham. After the round was over, one of the other pros approached the golfer and asked, "Hey, what was it like playing with the President and Billy Graham?" The pro unleashed a few choice curse words before saying, "I don't need Billy Graham stuffing religion down my throat!"[52] With that he headed to the practice tee to hit balls. His friend followed him. After allowing the pro to strike a few balls, the friend softly asked, "Was Billy a little rough on you out there?" The pro let out a humiliated sigh and said, "No, he didn't even mention religion. I just had a bad round."[53]

Graham never voiced a word about God, Jesus, or religion, yet the golf pro accused him ramming religion down his throat. Why? The pro golfer was reacting, not to Graham's speech, but to the presence of the Holy Spirit and the fruits of holiness in his life. Graham had girded himself with the armor of God, and in doing so, approached every situation clad like a soldier with a purpose, not like a bystander ready to take it all in. Martin Luther, the German reformer, cites: "The pagan does tremble at the rustling of a leaf. He feels the hound of Heaven breathing down his neck. He feels crowded by holiness even if it is only made present by an imperfect, partially sanctified human vessel."[54]

Lace up the Sandals of Peace

Sandals in the ancient Roman Empire were open-toed leather boots with thick, nail-studded soles, which were tied to the ankles and shins with straps. These were not running shoes for fleeing from or pursuing an enemy. In fact, Josephus tells of a centurion who, because he was running after his enemies while wearing "shoes thickly studded with sharp nails," slipped and fell on stone pavement, where he was duly dispatched.[55] In the same way football cleats are used for traction on the field, these boots gave soldiers an advantage on soft turf, enabling them to hold ground against an assaulting army.

I knew I had met someone special when I met Kandi, my wife, but my respect for her went to a whole new level during the Summer of 2004. She traveled to Glorieta, New Mexico the summer I served as camp pastor. On one of those vacation days my parents decided that we should visit the mountains where the Mayans once resided. Kandi thought, as I did, that we were going to look at the mountains from a distance, but that was not the case. My parents decided, without telling us, that we would climb the jagged terrain. They prepared with proper footwear for the upcoming hike; Kandi didn't.

She was not wearing tennis shoes like the rest of us; rather, she wore high heels that matched her stunning sundress. She was always beautiful, but there is something especially eye-catching about your girlfriend traversing the side of a mountain in high heels. As I followed her, I chuckled as the people coming down the mountain passed by us with their heads on a swivel.

Neither Kandi nor I knew my parents were planning on mountain climbing that day. The difference, however, was that I wore my black Doc Martins with rubber soles; Kandi, we immediately realized, did not. Appropriate footwear is essential for climbing and battle. Did you know that we are encouraged to put on a certain type of shoe in our battle against Satan? What are we standing on? Steve Maddens, Doc Martins, or Nikes? No! We are to stand firm upon the gospel.

Through the gospel of Jesus Christ we are firmly planted

in peace with God. "Therefore, since we have been declared righteous by faith, we have peace with God through our Lord Jesus Christ" (Romans 5:1). Jesus came to the earth to appease the wrath of a holy God. His death, burial, and resurrection provided access to Him. *We have rest for our restless souls when our soles are grounded in the peace of Christ.*

Take Up the Shield of Faith

The shield was used for protection of the body — the heart, lungs, and other vital organs. The average shield during the time of Paul's writing measured four feet in length by one-and-a-half feet in width. It was composed with two layers of laminated wood bound top and bottom with iron. The oblong form was covered with reinforced leather at the top and bottom. It was designed to protect the soldier against arrows. The shield could also extinguish flaming darts that were sometimes hurled at an army.

Paul uses vivid warfare imagery to depict the protective gear. Our Christian lives are replete with examples of the enemy launching fiery darts at us — deception, discouragement, lies, and temptations — to lead us into sin and, in so doing, bring about our demise. But we respond by having faith in God and His Word, standing on His promises, and not being swayed in our thinking. The arrows are harmless to us, for faith is our shield of protection.

Most things we do are by faith. You visit a doctor whose name you cannot pronounce, where he gives you a prescription you cannot read. You hand it to a pharmacist you have never seen before who provides you medicine you are unfamiliar with, and you take it willingly. All of this is done in sincere faith.

Do you demonstrate the same faith in God? Is your faith ultimately in God or yourself? The reason these questions are important is because we are not protected from the devil by our own strength. Instead, we are protected against the evil one because of our relationship with and trust in God.

PowerAde, the sports drink company, initiated a campaign around the story of David and Goliath. They boasted, "Goliath had size, but David's got game." Unfortunately, the tantalizing title is only partly correct. David didn't have game; he had God. When David battled Goliath, he came to victory because he rejected conventional wisdom and weaponry for the hand of God. Consider 1 Samuel 17:45-47:

> *David said to the Philistine: "You come against me with a dagger, spear, and sword, but I come against you in the name of Yahweh of Hosts, the God of Israel's armies—you have defied Him. Today, the Lord will hand you over to me. Today, I'll strike you down, cut your head off, and give the corpses of the Philistine camp to the birds of the sky and the creatures of the earth. Then all the world will know that Israel has a God, and this whole assembly will know that it is not by sword or by spear that the Lord saves, for the battle is the Lord's. He will hand you over to us."*

We should live like David who stepped on the battlefield with five smooth stones, dependent upon God for the victory. Victory is ours through Christ if we merely appropriate the promises of Scripture.

Wear the Helmet of Salvation

Paul borrows the metaphor "helmet of salvation" from Isaiah 59:17: "He put on righteousness like a breastplate, and a helmet of salvation on His head; He put on garments of vengeance for clothing, and He wrapped Himself in zeal as in a cloak." In the context of Isaiah 59, God put on the helmet, but in Ephesians the believer receives the helmet. The word "take" means "to accept something." Just as a helmet is issued to a soldier by his supply officer before entering battle, salvation is offered to Christians by God as a gift of protection: "For you have been saved by grace through faith…" (Ephesians 2:8).

Ancient helmets of this period were made of brass and iron. They offered the greatest protection possible for the day. The helmet not only protects, it also boosts morale. Have you ever watched an eight year old play football? Before the helmet, he lacks confidence, but after he puts on his helmet, something changes. He turns into a wrecking ball with legs. Just like a child with a helmet, we can have confidence as a result of the salvation God has given us. This is why assurance of salvation is an indispensable doctrine of the faith. If you're still not sure about your salvation, go back and reread the first two chapters of this book. Without assurance, believers are defenseless against the enemy.

Most of the people reading this book are blessed to live in one of the greatest countries in the world—the United States of America. Our government spends billions of dollars protecting us from outside attacks. We have a global military presence with infrared radar, drones, stealth bombers, ships, submarines, and weapons of mass destruction. Our intelligence services track the movement of anyone seeking to attack this country. Local police install fences with barbed wire, as well as cameras, alarm systems, and locks to keep the "bad guys" out of our borders. All of this is well and good. But what precautions are we taking to protect the morals of our society and values of our families? Christian values are being attacked in schools, universities, courtrooms, and churches. Our country is anything but prepared for the rampant paganism that plagues our land. The enemy pounces on unpreparedness.

On one occasion, Martin Luther, when he thought he was engaged in a spiritual attack, felt as if the devil was accusing him of his many sins. Luther imagined that Satan presented him with a long list of transgressions, reading them all aloud from the top. When Satan had finished, Luther replied, "Think a little harder. You must have forgotten some." The devil added more accusations to the list until he could come up with nothing else. Luther calmly said, "That's fine. Now write across that long list in red ink, 'The blood of Jesus Christ, His Son, cleanses me from all sin.'" It was after that statement that the devil departed.[56]

Christian, the battle has been won for us! We are never commanded to attack the devil; we are merely promised that if we "stand firm," he will flee. Take hold of your shield, put on your helmet, and take a stance against the encroaching evil forces of this world.

Wield the Sword of the Spirit

It is not the Spirit that is our sword, but the gospel; the Spirit sharpens the blade. The writer of Hebrews, speaking in the same vein, explains, "For the word of God is living and effective and sharper than any double-edged sword, penetrating as far as the separation of soul and spirit, joints and marrow. It is able to judge the ideas and thoughts of the heart" (Hebrews 4:12). Paul's reference to "the word" in Ephesians is synonymous with the gospel message. The mention of the "word" in this section is commonly used to describe a prophetic utterance or teaching, i.e., the message of the gospel.

Every person is in need of the gospel. Because of the sin of Adam, the human race has been infected with sin. Sin has to be punished for God to remain just. If we die in our sinful nature, we pay the price for our sins, and the wages of sin is death. But God offered a solution to our sin problem before He even created the world. He sent His Son, wrapped in human flesh, on a rescue mission to save mankind. Jesus lived a sinless life, died in our place, was raised from the dead, and ascended into heaven, where He now sits at the right hand of the Father.

Everyone who rejects the salvation that is offered through Christ will be banished to hell for eternity, but anyone who repents and believes in Christ will be forgiven of his or her sins, adopted into the family of God, given the resources of heaven, filled with the Spirit, and secured a place in heaven forever. Faith is established by the Word: "So faith comes from what is heard, and what is heard comes through the message about Christ" (Romans 10:17). By the Word, hardened hearts are melted, rebel sinners are made repentant, lost men and women are called to their new home, and Satan is defeated. Martin Luther, knowing this truth well, penned these words in the great hymn, *A Mighty Fortress:*

And though this world, with devils filled, should threaten to undo us,

We will not fear, God hath willed his truth to triumph through us.

The Prince of Darkness grim, we tremble not for him;

His rage we can endure, for lo, his doom is sure;

One little Word shall fell him.[57]

Understanding the enemy is but the first step in the process of overcoming our enemy. The next step is to prepare oneself for the fight that is to come.

Questions to Consider

Why is every piece of the armor vital to spiritual warfare? Why is only knowing about the armor insufficient when facing temptation? In other words, what good is armor that is only stored in a closet?

Preparing for the Battle

There are several practical ways a believer can prepare for battle. First, we must "put on Christ" by living like He did (Romans 13:14). Paul likens putting on Christ in Romans 13:12 with wearing the armor of light. He uses the same imagery in Colossians 3:10-12, where he instructs believers to "put on the new self" — to live in a manner that is pleasing to God — and again in Ephesians 4:24, where he states, "put on the new self, the one created according to God's likeness in righteousness and purity of the truth." Believers prepare for the battle before the battle begins, not in the thick of the warfare. The first step is to clothe yourself as a soldier who has been given a specific purpose, something to focus on—obedience to the orders of the Commander in charge.

Second, we must saturate our lives with the Word of God. Our discipleship ministry, Replicate, recently developed a reading plan called the F-260 (Foundational 260), which is a plan outlining 260 essential passages from the Old and New Testaments that every disciple of Christ should be familiar with (see Appendix 2 for a copy of the plan). We recently developed an app for your iPhone that works in conjunction with the reading plan by offering weekly Scripture memory verses (visit replicateministries.org for more information). Each verse coincides with the weeks reading. Believers must get into the Word until the Word gets into them. Reading and memorizing are powerful ways to respond to temptation. Jesus fended off Satan during His temptation by quoting the Word repeatedly (Matthew 4:1-11).

Finally, we can spend time meditating on the Word. Meditation is a word that scares many believers, but in reality, it holds one of the great secrets of becoming a great man or woman of the faith. Hudson Taylor, the founder of China Inland Mission, overcame immense hardships with daily meditation on God's Word:

> It was not easy for Mr. Taylor, in his changeful life, to make time for prayer and Bible study, but he knew that it was vital. Many remembered traveling with him month after month in northern China, by cart and wheelbarrow with the poorest of inns at night, often with only one large room for travelers to fit in. They would screen off a corner for their father and another for themselves, with curtains of some sort; and then after sleep at last had brought a measure of quiet, they would hear a match struck and see the flicker of candlelight by Mr. Taylor. Although he was weary, he poured over the little Bible in two volumes always at hand. From two to four a.m. was the time he usually gave to prayer and study; the time he could be most sure of being undisturbed to wait upon God.[58]

One word sums up this chapter — *readiness*. Put on the armor of God, wield the sword with all courage, and go forth in the grace of God. The battle has been won, so stand firm!

Points to Consider

Are there situations in your life that would have been different had you been "suited up" or in a state of readiness? How can you begin to change this today?

Chapter 10

Calling Out to the Commander in Chief

Spiritual Warfare II

After four arduous years of war and countless experiments, President Harry S. Truman issued the order to drop the atomic bomb on August 6, 1945. United States troops on board a B-29 bomber, the *Enola Gay*, released the first nuclear bomb, nicknamed "Little Boy," on Hiroshima, Japan. One minute later, the bomb exploded with a magnitude that had never been felt or seen before. Three days later, another bomb was dropped on Nagasaki which ultimately brought a decisive end to years of death and destruction during World War II. Although America had the capability to drop the bomb years earlier, our military waited to drop it years into battle. Sometimes in battle, the situation calls for the most powerful element we have in our arsenal. In the battle against the spiritual forces of the enemy, the most powerful weapon at our disposal is often the one we pull out last — prayer.

Even though we are discussing it in the final chapter, it is of first importance. In the previous chapter, Paul described the armament of a warrior in the army of the Lord. Regardless of how well a disciple wears truth, righteousness, faith, salvation, and peace, and no matter how well they wield the Word, *prayer must be a priority*. Edward Payson said, "Prayer is the first thing, the second thing, the third thing necessary to minister. Pray, therefore my dear brothers, pray, pray, pray."[59] Success in the battle depends upon our ability to pray and the frequency of our prayers.

Question to Consider

How would you rate your prayer life?

Participate in the Battle by Praying for Believers

One of the most important ways one can wield the weapon of prayer in battle is to pray for other believers: "Pray at all times in the Spirit with every prayer and request, and stay alert in this with all perseverance and intercession for all the saints" (Ephesians 6:18). The terms "pray" and "stay alert" are not commands but participles: verb forms used to modify nouns. Some have suggested prayer to be the seventh piece of our armor. This is highly unlikely because Paul never mentions prayer as a piece of equipment you put on or hold on to. Instead, prayer permeates every aspect of one's life. Prayer connects to the main exhortation issued earlier in verse 14 — "stand." It is foundational for the deployment of weapons and for fortifying ourselves with spiritual armor. Did you notice the four "alls" in the passage? Most Christians pray infrequently, with a minimal degree of perseverance, for some of God's people. But Paul modifies the "prayers" of believers with the word "all," thereby introducing a new dimension of prayer.

The Responsibility to Pray: All Prayer and Supplication

The most common Greek word for "prayer" in the New Testament envisions a person petitioning God for something. The word "supplication" is synonymous with the word "petition."

Notice how many times Paul uses a form of this word in Ephesians 6:18: "praying," "all prayer," "supplication," and "making supplication." Paul uses repetition to stress the importance of prayer in a believer's life. You must pray continually because the evil forces against us never rest. Satan never sleeps. The spiritual forces of evil never take a ceasefire. Paul, in essence, is saying, "Praying always with all prayer." These prayers are zealous prayers, weeping prayers, prayers consisting of a single word, prayers without a word being mentioned, prayers for others, prayers of confession, and prayers of thanksgiving. We must pray continuously with all prayer and supplication.

The Rate of Prayer: All Times in the Spirit

We should be praying "at all times in the Spirit." Prayer is not confined to a church building or a prayer closet. Believers pray in the Spirit. What does it mean to pray "in the Spirit"? Paul does not have in mind praying in tongues, as some have wrongly interpreted this passage. Even those who claim to speak in tongues would agree that it is impossible to pray in tongues "all the time." Praying in the Spirit is to pray in harmony with and according to the will of God. We are dependent upon the Holy Spirit to guide and direct our lives. He energizes us in prayer. He nudges us to pray for certain family members, missionaries, pastors, leaders, etc. He sustains us in prayer. Here are three passages about "praying in the Spirit":

- For you did not receive a spirit of slavery to fall back into fear, but you received the Spirit of adoption, by whom we cry out, *"Abba, Father!"* The Spirit Himself testifies together with our spirit that we are God's children *(Romans 8:15-16)*.
- In the same way the Spirit also joins to help in our weakness, because we do not know what to pray for as we should, but the Spirit Himself intercedes for us with unspoken groanings *(Romans 8:26)*.
- But you, dear friends, as you build yourselves up in your most holy faith and pray in the Holy Spirit, keep yourselves in the love

of God, expecting the mercy of our Lord Jesus Christ for eternal life *(Jude 20-21).*

Praying in the Spirit aligns us with God's will, while enveloping us with the love of God. We cannot keep ourselves in the love of God; He keeps us. Jude 1 says, "To those who are called, loved by God the Father and *kept* by Jesus Christ" (emphasis mine). Jude continues in verse 24, "Now to Him who is able to protect you from stumbling and to make you stand in the presence of His glory, blameless and with great joy." Who does the keeping? God does. So here is the conundrum: how are we able to keep *ourselves*, which is a command from Paul, if God is doing the keeping? We carry out this command through prayer. We ask God to keep us from stumbling in prayer, and He does so through the Spirit. We should not view this as casual prayer, but an exercise we engage in often. Consider the following illustration about the power of prayer:

During one of Dr. Wilbur Chapman's campaigns in England, the attendance was consistently low. He received word that an American missionary was going to pray for him. Almost instantly the hall became packed, and at his first invitation, fifty men accepted Christ as Savior. One night the missionary was in the congregation. When Dr. Chapman was introduced to him, he asked him to pray for him. The two went to Dr. Chapman's room, dropped on their knees, and for five minutes the missionary was quiet. "I could hear my heart thumping," Chapman said. "I felt hot tears running down my face. I knew I was with God." Then the missionary said, "O God!" and was silent for another five minutes. When he knew he was talking with God, there came from the depth of his heart such petitions for men, as I have never heard before.

When Chapman rose from his knees, he knew what prayer was. He realized afterward that the missionary was Praying Hyde. John Hyde knew the power of supplication in the Spirit because he spent hours each day in prayer. By 1899, he began spending entire nights face down before God. In a letter to his college he wrote: "I have felt led to pray for others this winter as never before. I never before knew what it was to work all day and then pray all night before God for another.... In college or at parties at home, I used to keep such hours for myself, or pleasure, and can I not do as much for God and souls?"[60]

Point to Ponder

Do you view prayer as an event or as a never-ending conversation with God?

The Resolve of Prayer: All Perseverance and Alertness

We must be prayerfully alert to what is happening in our home, neighborhood, city, country, and world. Paul reminds us to stay "alert with all perseverance, making supplication for all the saints." This verse reminds us of Jesus' words shortly before His arrest: "Then He came and found them sleeping. 'Simon, are you sleeping?' He asked Peter. 'Couldn't you stay awake one hour? Stay awake and pray so that you won't enter into temptation. The spirit is willing, but the flesh is weak.'" (Mark 14:37-38). The tense of the word "watch" gives us the impression that Jesus kept repeating His warning: "Watch and pray!" Jesus expected them to be on guard against temptation, yet He found them sleeping in the garden. How about you? *Have you been sleeping in the garden?* Or have you been standing guard in prayer?

Sadly, there is great activity in the world, great movements, great meetings, great ideas, but no persistent prayer. E.M. Bounds, in his classic work on prayer, suggested that "the [prayer] closet is not an asylum for the lazy and worthless Christian. It is not a nursery where none but babes belong. It is the battlefield of the

Church, it's the Citadel."[61] Bounds went on to record the prayer lives of great men of the faith:

- Charles Simeon "devoted the hours of four till eight in the morning to God."
- John Wesley "spent two hours daily in prayer. He began at four in the morning."
- John Fletcher would pray throughout the night on many occasions. "I would not rise from my seat," commented Fletcher, "without lifting my heart to God."
- Martin Luther stated, "If I fail to spend two hours in prayer each morning, the devil gets the victory through the day. I have so much business I cannot get on without spending three hours daily in prayer."
- Bishop Ken, enamored by the grace of God in his life, would arise before three a.m. every morning.
- Bishop Asbury stated, "I propose to rise at four o'clock as often as I spend two hours in prayer and meditation."
- Joseph Alleine woke up around four o'clock every morning to spend time praying until eight a.m. If he heard others up working before him, he would cry out to God, "O how this shames me. Does not my master deserve more than theirs."
- Bishop Andrews devoted more than five hours every day in prayer and devotion.
- Adoniram Judson's effectiveness in India is attributed to prayer. He said, "Arrange thy affairs if possible so that thou can leisurely devote two or three hours every day not merely to devotional exercises but to the very act of secret prayer and communion with God. Endeavor seven times a day to withdraw from business and company and lift up thy soul to God in private retirement. Begin the day by rising after midnight and devoting some time amid the silence and darkness of the night to this sacred work. Let the hours of nine, twelve, three, six and nine at night witness the same."[62]

Question to Consider

*Who needs prayer in your life? Make
a list of people you can pray for.*

How many times have we given up on God because He didn't move immediately? We must continue to pray, and pray, and pray, and pray. Do you know anyone who does not know Jesus? Pray for them. Do you know anyone in your family who is in the middle of a spiritual attack? Pray for them. Do you know someone who needs healing, assistance, or freedom from sin? Pray for them.

Pray before you begin your day. Pray on your way to school or work. Pray when you arrive and thank God for getting you there safely. Pray for assistance from the Spirit throughout the day. Pray on the drive home. Pray before you eat any meal. Pray before you retire to bed. Pray now and pray often!

The Recipients of Prayer: All Saints

Who are the saints? Are these only those individuals who have been set apart by the Church? Are these the special men and women who are spiritually superior to ordinary believers? To both of these questions, the answer is "No." The word "saints" is another word for believers — all of them. The term appears sixty-one times in the New Testament, and forty-one times by Paul alone. Examine how Paul uses the word "saints":

- Romans 1:7: "To all who are in Rome, loved by God, called as *saints.*"
- Romans 15:25 "Right now I am traveling to Jerusalem to serve the *saints…*"
- 1 Corinthians 1:2: "To God's church at Corinth, to those who are sanctified in Christ Jesus and called as *saints*, with all

those in every place who call on the name of Jesus Christ our Lord — both their Lord and ours."

- Ephesians 1:1: "To the faithful *saints* in Christ Jesus at Ephesus."
- Philippians 1:1: "To all the *saints* in Christ Jesus who are in Philippi, including the overseers and deacons."

In the Catholic Church in which I was raised, saints are men and women who have died with an extra measure of grace upon their lives. Therefore, parishioners are challenged to pray to them in order to receive that extra grace. Biblical prayer for the saints is quite different. Notice Paul doesn't pray *to* the saints. Instead, he prays *for* the saints.

So for whom should we pray? We aren't to pray a superficial blanketed prayer for believers around the world. Think about missionaries serving overseas, ministry leaders that you know, pastors at your church, believers in your Sunday Bible Study class, and family members who know Christ. Pray for what? That they might be healthy, wealthy, or happy? Better yet, pray that they might speak the gospel boldly for the development of the kingdom of God!

The Request of the Prayer: Boldness

Although prayer can be applied to different areas of one's life, Paul suggests that we should request something specific: *boldness*. Imagine this is your life after surrendering to ministry:

I have worked harder, been put in prison more often, been whipped times without number, and faced death again and again. Five different times the Jewish leaders gave me thirty-nine lashes. Three times I was beaten with rods. Once I was stoned. Three times I was shipwrecked. Once I spent a whole night and a day adrift at sea. I have traveled on many long journeys. I have faced danger from rivers and from robbers. I have faced danger from my own people, the Jews, as well as from the Gentiles. I have faced danger in the cities, in the deserts, and on the seas. And I have faced danger from men who claim to be believers but are not. I have worked hard and long, enduring many sleepless nights. I have been hungry and thirsty and have often gone without food. I have shivered in the cold, without enough clothing to keep me warm. Then, besides all this, I have the daily burden of my concern for all the churches. Who is weak without my feeling that weakness? Who is led astray, and I do not burn with anger? (2 Corinthians 11:23-28, NLT).

Imagine that you are currently imprisoned for preaching the gospel. For what are you asking people to pray? Are you asking them to pray that the Lord might rescue you from prison, exonerate you of all charges, or bring pain upon your captors? No. If you are anything like Paul, you request prayer "that the message may be given to me when I open my mouth to make known with boldness the mystery of the gospel. For this I am an ambassador in chains. Pray that I might be bold enough in Him to speak as I should" (Ephesians 6:19-20). God was using Paul in prison, so it was in prison Paul wished to stay.

Paul witnessed firsthand the effects of his boldness in prison: "Now I want you to know, brothers, that what has happened to me has actually resulted in the advance of the gospel, so that it has become known throughout the whole imperial guard, and to everyone else, that my imprisonment is in the cause of Christ. Most of the brothers in the Lord have gained confidence from my imprisonment and dare even more to speak the message fearlessly" (Philippians 1:12-14). Paul desires the readers to pray that words may be given to him when he opens his mouth to share the gospel. He yearns to make known the gospel with clarity and simplicity in spite of his imprisonment.

A measure of irony is evident in his previous statement: "I am an ambassador in chains that I may declare it boldly, as I ought to speak." Author Markus Barth explains, "The term 'chain' signifies among other things the (golden) adornment(s) worn around the neck and wrists by rich ladies or high-ranking men. On festive occasions, ambassadors wear such chains in order to reveal the riches, power, and dignity of the government they represent. Because Paul serves Christ crucified, he considers the painful iron prison chains as the most appropriate insignia for the representation of his Lord."[63] What concerns Paul most is not that his wrists may be unchained, but that his mouth may be metaphorically unchained to share the testimony of Christ.

Question to Consider

In what areas of your life do you need more boldness to share the gospel, i.e. work, family, friends, etc? Pray specifically for those areas.

The suffering of Christian exiles from Bohemia and Moravia bothered Count Nikolaus Ludwig von Zinzendorf so much that in 1722 he moved to establish a community on his estate in Germany to house them. The center, known as "Herrnhut," grew quickly, and so did its appreciation for the power of prayer. On August 27, 1727, twenty-four men and women agreed to devote one hour each day in scheduled prayer around the clock. Soon others joined the prayer chain. Days passed, then months. Unceasing prayer rose to God twenty-four hours a day, seven days a week. The intercessors met weekly for encouragement and to read letters and messages from their brothers and sisters abroad. The Herrnhut prayer meeting lasted more than a hundred years. Without question, the prayer chain assisted in birthing the Protestant missions movement.

Zinzendorf, twenty-seven years old at the time, set his sights on reaching the West Indies, Greenland, Turkey, and Lapland with the gospel. Twenty-six Moravians answered his call to forsake comforts and normalcy for unchartered territory. Twenty-two missionaries died and two more were imprisoned during the first two years. However, others were eager to replace them on the field. The Moravians' unwavering commitment to the advancement of the Great Commission influenced the conversions of John and Charles Wesley and implicitly sparked the Great Awakenings that swept through America and Europe. A total of seventy Moravian missionaries were commissioned from the community to serve in various places around the globe. Only God knows the spiritual impact this hundred-year prayer meeting had on this earth.[64]

Let Us Pray

Let me offer two practices for believers to participate in prayer. First, pray at particular times of the day. If you need to exercise discipline in your prayer life, choose a specific time every day that you will not be distracted and devote yourself to God in prayer. Set an alarm on your phone, mark it on your calendar, or just make the effort to pray daily. If possible, write down pertinent things for which you wish to pray. Pray for those closest to you: your spouse, kids, parents, and extended family. Pray for people in your local church: pastors, leaders, and Sunday Bible study teachers. Pray for people in ministry: missionaries and evangelists. But don't forget to pray for those closest to you who are not saved that the Spirit would cultivate in them the faith necessary to approach God humbly for forgiveness and restoration.

Second, practice the presence of God. Early on in my Christian life, I sought a way to pray without ceasing as Paul suggests in 1 Thessalonians 5:17. The question I kept asking was, "Is it possible to carry on a continuous verbal dialogue with the Lord throughout the day?" Thomas Kelley in his book, *Testament of Devotion,* says "yes." He writes: "There is a way of ordering our mental life on more than one level at once. On one level, we can be thinking, discussing, seeing, calculating, and meeting all the demands of external affairs. But deep within, behind the scenes, at a profounder level, we may also be in prayer and adoration, song and worship, and a gentle receptiveness to divine breathings."[65] Though we may not be able to carry on a running dialogue with God, we can be mindful of His presence.

As a new believer, I stumbled upon a book entitled, *The Practice of the Presence of God*. A medieval monk named Brother Lawrence wrote this little book, ninety-one pages in all. He outlined his experiences of intimacy with God at all times. "The time of business does not differ with me from the time of prayer," writes Lawrence, "and in the noise and clatter of my kitchen, while several persons are at the same time calling for different things, I possess God in as great tranquility as if I were on my knees."[66] Whether he was cooking or cleaning, walking or working, God was on Brother Lawrence's mind. Likewise, Paul encouraged every believer to practice consistent prayer. Whether you are a business owner, stay-at-home mom, factory worker, student, or salesman, you can implement this discipline in your life. You should practice setting your mind's attention and heart's affection on the Lord continuously.

Encouragement and Hope for the Future

As we draw this discussion to a close, it is fitting to offer you encouragement and hope in your journey to make disciples who make disciples. I want to inspire you to press on, because you are in the middle of the journey God created for you to endure. I want to remind you of the hope you have in Christ. All people, regardless of age, race, color, or creed, are treasured by a God who longs for communion with them. Some are at the beginning of this journey, while others have been walking for many years by now. But if you are reading this, the journey is not over. Your past doesn't predict your future. The final chapter of your life is yet to be written. Seek hard after God and fix your gaze upon Christ.

You'll be glad you did!

Points to Ponder

Soldiers today have the luxury of fighting wars with the advantage of aerial surveillance. Believers have the blessing of direct communication with God during spiritual warfare. Are you taking advantage of staying connected with God during spiritual warfare? If so, how?

APPENDIX 1

FAITH DECLARATION

The Book of Ephesians

Affirm Your Position and Practice In Christ

I have been blessed with every spiritual blessing (Ephesians 1:3)

I have been chosen before the foundation of the world (1:4a)

I am holy and blameless (1:4b)

I have been predestined and adopted in love (1:5)

I have redemption through Christ's blood, the forgiveness of my trespasses (1:7)

I have obtained an inheritance in heaven (1:10)

I have been sealed with the Holy Spirit of promise (1:13)

I have been made spiritually alive together with Christ (2:5)

I have been seated in Christ in the heavenly places (2:6)

I have been saved by God's grace through faith (2:8)

I have become God's workmanship, created in Christ Jesus for good works (2:10)

I have been brought near to God by the blood of Christ, and Christ Himself is my peace (2:13-14)

I have access to God through Christ (2:18)

I am no longer a stranger and alien, but a fellow citizen with the saints and a member of God's household (2:19)

I am a fellow heir and fellow member of the body of Christ and a fellow partaker of the promise in Christ Jesus through the gospel (3:6)

I have boldness and confident access to God through faith in Christ (3:12)

Therefore,

I will walk in a manner worthy of the calling with which I have been called (4:1)

I will use my spiritual gifts in the work of service, to the building up of the body of Christ (4:12)

I will no longer walk as the Gentiles' walk-in the futility of their mind (4:17)

I will lay aside the old self and put on the new self through the renewing of my mind (4:4:23-24)

I will lay aside falsehood and speak truth (4:25)

I will be angry at sin, and yet, not sin in my anger (4:26)

I will not give the devil an opportunity (4:27)

I will steal no longer, but labor so that I will have something to share with those in need (4:28)

No unwholesome word will proceed from my mouth, but only words that edify (4:29)

I will not grieve the Holy Spirit of God (4:30)

I put away all bitterness, wrath, anger, clamor, slander, and all malice (4:31)

I will be kind, tender-hearted, and forgiving (4:32)

I will imitate God the Father as a beloved child and walk in love (5:1)

I will walk as a child of Light-in all goodness, righteousness, and truth (5:8-9)

I will not participate in the unfruitful deeds of darkness, but rather expose them (5:11)

I will walk in wisdom, making the most of my time because the days are evil (5:15-16)

I will be filled with the Holy Spirit (5:18)

I will be subject to those in authority in the fear of Christ (5:21)

I will be strong in the Lord and in the strength of His might (6:10)

I will pray at all times in the Spirit (6:18)

APPENDIX 2
FOUNDATIONAL 260 (F-260)

Week 1
Genesis 1 -2
Genesis 3-4
Genesis 6-7
Genesis 8-9
Job 1-2
MV: Genesis 1:27
Hebrews 11:7

Week 2
Job 38-39
Job 40-42
Genesis 11-12
Genesis 15
Genesis 16-17
MV: Hebrews 11:8-10;
11:6

Week 3
Genesis 18-19
Genesis 20-21
Genesis 22
Genesis 24
Genesis 25:19-34; 26

MV: Romans 4:20-22;
Hebrews 11:17-19

Week 4
Genesis 27-28
Genesis 29-30:24
Genesis 31-32
Genesis 33 & 35
Genesis 37
MV: 2 Corinthians
10:12; 1 John 3:18

Week 5
Genesis 39-40
Genesis 41
Genesis 42-43
Genesis 44-45
Genesis 46-47
MV: Ephesians 3:20-
21; Romans 8:28-30

Week 6
Genesis 48-49
Genesis 50 – Exodus 1

Exodus 2-3
Exodus 4-5
Exodus 6-7
MV: Genesis 50:20;
Hebrews 11:24-26

Week 7
Exodus 8-9
Exodus 10-11
Exodus 12
Exodus 13:17-14
Exodus 16-17
MV: John 1:29;
Hebrews 9:22

Week 8
Exodus 19-20 Ten
Commandments
Exodus 24-25
Exodus 26-27
Tabernacle
Exodus 28-29
Tabernacle

Exodus 30-31
Tabernacle
MV: 10
Commandments

Week 9
Exodus 32-33
Exodus 34-36:1
Exodus 40
Leviticus 8-9
Leviticus 16-17
MV: Exodus 33:16;
Matthew 22:37-39

Week 10
Leviticus 23
Leviticus 26
Numbers 11-12
Numbers 13-14
Numbers 16-17
MV: Leviticus 26:13;
Deuteronomy 31:7-8

Week 11
Numbers 20; 27:12-23
Numbers 34-35
Deuteronomy 1-2
Deuteronomy 3-4
Deuteronomy 6-7
MV: Deuteronomy
4:7; 6: 4-9

Week 12
Deuteronomy 8-9
Deuteronomy 30-31
Deuteronomy 32:48-52; 34
Joshua 1-2
Joshua 3-4
MV: Joshua 1:8-9;
Psalm 1:1-2

Week 13
Joshua 5:10-15; 6
Joshua 7-8
Joshua 23-24
Judges 2-3
Judges 4
MV: Joshua 24:14-15;
Judges 2:12

Week 14
Judges 6-7
Judges 13-14
Judges 15-16
Ruth 1-2
Ruth 3-4
MV: Galatians 4:4-5;
Psalm 19:14

Week 15
1 Samuel 1-2
1 Samuel 3; 8
1 Samuel 9-10
1 Samuel 13-14
1 Samuel 15-16
MV: 1 Samuel 15:22;
16:7

Week 16
1 Samuel 17-18
1 Samuel 19-20
1 Samuel 21-22
Psalm 22; 1 Samuel 24-25:1
1 Samuel 28; 31
MV: 1 Samuel
17:46-47;
2 Timothy 4:17

Week 17
2 Samuel 1; 2:1-7
2 Samuel 3:1; 5; Psalm 23
2 Samuel 6-7
Psalm 18; 2 Samuel 9
2 Samuel 11-12
MV: Psalms 23:1-3;
51:10-13

Week 18
Psalm 51
2 Samuel 24; Psalm 24
Psalms 1; 19
Psalms 103; 119:1-48
Psalm 119:49-128
MV: Psalms 1:1-7;
119:7-11

Week 19
Psalms 119:129-176; 139
Psalms 148-150
1 Kings 2
1 Kings 3; 6

1 Kings 8; 9:1-9
**MV: Psalms 139:1-3;
139:15-16**
Week 20
Proverbs 1-2
Proverbs 3-4
Proverbs 16-18
Proverbs 31
1 Kings 11-12
**MV: Proverbs 1:7;
3:5-6**

Week 21
1 Kings 16:29-34; 17
1 Kings 18-19
1 Kings 21-22
2 Kings 2
2 Kings 5; 6:1-23
MV: Psalm 63:1; 17:15

Week 22
Jonah 1-2
Jonah 3-4
Hosea 1-3
Amos 1:1; 9
Joel 1-3
**MV: Psalm 16:11;
John 11:25-26**

Week 23
Isaiah 6; 9
Isaiah 44-45
Isaiah 52-53
Isaiah 65-66
Micah 1; 4:6-13; 5

**MV: Isaiah 53:5-6; 1
Peter 2:23-24**

Week 24
2 Kings 17-18
2 Kings 19-21
2 Kings 22-23
Jeremiah 1-3:5
Jeremiah 25; 29
**MV: Proverbs 29:18;
Jeremiah 1:15**

Week 25
Jeremiah 31:31-40;
32-33
Jeremiah 52; 2 Kings
24-25
Ezekiel 1:1-3; 36:16-38;
37
Daniel 1-2
Daniel 3
**MV: Ezekiel 36:26-27;
Psalm 51:10**

Week 26
Daniel 5-6
Daniel 9-10; 12
Ezra 1-2
Ezra 3-4
Ezra 5-6
**MV: Daniel 6:26-27;
9:19**

Week 27
Zechariah 1:1-6; 2; 12
Ezra 7-8
Ezra 9-10
Esther 1-2
Esther 3-4
**MV: Zephaniah 3:17;
1 Peter 3:15**

Week 28
Esther 5-7
Esther 8-10
Nehemiah 1-2
Nehemiah 3-4
Nehemiah 5-6
**MV: Deuteronomy
29:29; Psalms 101:3-4**

Week 29
Nehemiah 7-8
Nehemiah 9
Nehemiah 10
Nehemiah 11
Nehemiah 12
**MV: Nehemiah 9:6;
Colossians 1:15-16**

Week 30
Nehemiah 13
Malachi 1
Malachi 2
Malachi 3
Malachi 4
**MV: Psalm 51:17;
Colossians 1:19-20**

Week 31
Luke 1
Luke 2
Matthew 1-2
Mark 1
John 1
MV: John 1:1-2; 14

Week 32
Matthew 2-4
Matthew 5
Matthew 6
Matthew 7
Matthew 8
MV: Matthew 5:16;
6:33

Week 33
Luke 9:10-62
Mark 9-10
Luke 12
John 3-4
Luke 14
MV: Luke 14:26-27;
14:33

Week 34
John 6
Matthew 19:16-30
Luke 15-16
Luke 17:11-37; 18
Mark 10
MV: Mark 10:45;
John 6:37

Week 35
John 11; Matthew
21:1-13
John 13
John 14-15
John 16
Matt 24
MV: John 13:34-35;
15:4-5

Week 36
Matthew 24:1-46
John 17
Matthew 26:47-Matt.
27:31
Matthew 27:32-66;
Luke 23:26-56
John 19
MV: Luke 23:34; John
17:3

Week 37
Mark 16; Matthew 28
Luke 24
John 20-21
Matthew 28
Acts 1
MV: Matthew
28:18-20;
Acts 1:8

Week 38
Acts 2-3
Acts 4-5
Acts 6
Acts 7
Acts 8-9
MV: Acts 2:42; 4:31

Week 39
Acts 10-11
Acts 12
Acts 13-14
James 1-2
James 3-5
MV: James 1: 2-4;
2:17

Week 40
Acts 15-16
Galatians 1-3
Galatians 4-6
Acts 17-18:17
1 Thess. 1-2
MV: Acts 17:11;
17:24-25

Week 41
1 Thess. 3-5
2 Thess. 1-3
Acts 18-19
1 Cor. 1-2
1 Cor. 3-4
MV: 1 Corinthians
1:18; 1 Thessalonians
5:23-24

Firmly Planted

Week 42	Week 46	2 Corinthians
1 Cor. 4-5	Acts 20-21	5:17
1 Cor. 6-7	Acts 22-23	
1 Cor. 8-9	Acts 24-25	
1 Cor. 10-11	Acts 26-27	Week 50
1 Cor. 12-14	Acts 28	1 Timothy 1-3
MV: 1 Corinthians	**MV: Acts 20:24; 2**	1 Timothy 4-6
10:13; 13:13	**Corinthians 4:7-10**	2 Timothy 1-2
Week 43		2 Timothy 3-4
1 Cor. 15-16	Week 47	1 Peter 1-2
2 Cor. 1-2	Colossians 1-2	**MV: 2 Timothy 2:1-2;**
2 Cor. 3-4	Colossians 3-4	**2:15**
2 Cor. 5-6	Ephesians 1-2	
2 Cor. 7-8	Ephesians 3-4	Week 51
MV: Romans 1:16-17;	Ephesians 5-6	1 Peter 3-4
1 Corinthians 15:3-4	**MV: Ephesians 2:8-**	1 Peter 5; 1 John 1
	10; Colossians 2:6-7	1 John 2-3
		1 John 4-5
Week 44		Revelation 1
2 Cor. 9-10	Week 48	**MV: 1 Peter 2:11; 1**
2 Cor. 11-13	Philippians 1-2	**John 4:10-11**
Romans 1-2; Acts	Philippians 3-4	
20:1-3	Hebrews 1-2	
Romans 3-4	Hebrews 3-4	Week 52
Romans 5-6	Hebrews 5-6	Revelation 2
MV: Romans 4:20-22;	**MV: Philippians 3:7-**	Revelation 3
5:1	**8; Hebrews 4:14-16**	Revelation 19:6-20
		Revelation 21
		Revelation 22
Week 45	Week 49	**MV: Revelation 3:19;**
Romans 7-8	Hebrews 6-7	**21:3-4**
Romans 9-10	Hebrews 8-9	
Romans 11-12	Hebrews 10	
Romans 13-14	Hebrew 11	
Romans 15-16	Hebrews 12	
MV: **Romans 8:1;**	**MV: Galatians**	
12:1-2	**2:19-20;**	

ACKNOWLEDGMENTS

As with any book, the unseen efforts of those behind the scenes make it a reality. Tim LaFleur, Dave Wiley, Mollie Wiley, Paul Laso, and Kandi Gallaty met with me weekly to critique and organize the material. I couldn't have done it without your input and support. You worked tirelessly to assist me in making the deadline for publication.

I am grateful for the editorial insights from Hamilton Barber and Jake Pratt. You have shaped this book into what it is today. I am thankful for the observations and comments from my current discipleship groups: Steve, Tom, Sherman, Chris, Miguel, Richard, Chad, Rick, Jim, and Monte. Each of you offered practical insights.

I am grateful for the members of Brainerd Baptist Church who extend love to my family and me each week. Your constant prayers and support have spurred me on. Also, I want to thank Linda Brown, my administrative assistant, for investing countless hours typing, proofing, and printing pages.

I am thankful for my wife Kandi and my boys, Rig and Ryder, who encouraged me every step of the way. Kandi, your example in making disciples inspires me to be a disciple who makes disciples.

Finally, I am eternally grateful for the salvation I have in Christ. In 2002, Jesus forgave me of my sins, exchanged my old life for a new one, adopted me into the family of God, and set me on a path for His namesake. I have never gotten over being saved since that day.

ENDNOTES

1. *The Holy Bible: Holman Christian Standard Version* (Nashville: Holman, 2009).

2. *The Holy Bible: English Standard Version* (Wheaton: Standard Bible Society, 2001).

3. Mishnah, Pirke Avot 5:27. Quoted in Ann Spangler and Lois Tverberg, *Sitting at the Feet of Rabbi Jesus: How the Jewishness of Jesus Can Transform Your Faith* (Grand Rapids: Zondervan, 2009), Kindle Location 4183.

4. Alan Carr, "How Can I Know for Sure" http://www.sermonnote-book.org /new%20 testament/1%20John%205_1-13.htm. [Internet] (Accessed 10 August 2014).

5. Harry Ironside, "Angel of Light," The Net Bible http://classic.net. bible.org/illustration.php?id=300. [Internet] (Accessed 20 August 2014).

6. Christopher B. Adsit, *Personal Disciple-making: A Step-by-Step Guide for Leading a Christian From New Birth to Maturity* (Orlando, FL: Campus Crusade for Christ, 1996), 130-131.

7. Ibid., 131.

8. John MacArthur, "11 Tests of Genuine Salvation" http://www. gty.org/resources /Positions/P06/Is-It-Real.[Internet] Accessed 22 August 2014).

9. Adrian Rogers, *What Every Christian Ought to Know Day by Day* (Nashville: B & H Publishers, 2008), 70

10. John MacArthur, *Ephesians* (Chicago: Moody, 1986), 166.

11. Edward Falkener, *Ephesus and the Temple of Diana* (Open Library: FQ Publishing, 2010), 13.

12. John Eadie, *A Commentary on the Greek Text of the Epistle of Paul to the Ephesians* (London: Forgotten Books, 2012), 351.

13. Dallas Willard, "How Does the Disciple Live?" in *Radix Magazine* 34:3 (Spring 2009).

14. Philip G. Zimbardo, "Stanford Prison Experiment," http://www.prisonexp.org. [Internet] (Accessed 27 July 2014).

15. Miles J. Stanford, *The Green Letters: Principles of Spiritual Growth* (Grand Rapids: Zondervan, 1981), 31.

16. See George Eldon Ladd *The Gospel of the Kingdom: Scriptural Studies in the Kingdom of God* (Grand Rapids, MI: Eerdmans Publishers, 1959). Ladd popularized this concept in describing the kingdom of God as being "already/not yet," signifying its dual dimension.

17. Bolton, Samuel, *The True Bounds of Christian Freedom* (Carlisle: Banner of Truth, 1965), 26-27.

18. Quoted by Anthony Carter in "Sanctified by the Blood" http://www.ligonier.org/learn/articles/sanctified-by-the-blood. [Internet] (Accessed 10 July 2014).

19. Robert H. Mounce, *Romans* (Nashville: Holman, 1995), 154.

20. Leo J. Daugherty III, *Train Wreckers and Ghost Killers* http://www.koreanwar2.org/kwp2/usmckorea/PDF_Monographs/KoreanWar.TrainWreckers-GhostKillers.pdf. [Internet] (Accessed 18 August 2014).

21. Neil T. Anderson, *The Bondage Breaker* (Eugene: Harvest House, 2006), 72, 136.

22. Adrian Rogers, "Seven Reasons Why You Can't Be Lost," http://www.lwf.org/site /News2?abbr=for_&page=NewsArticle&id=6157. [Internet] (Accessed 10 June 2014).

23. Timothy George, *Galatians*, vol. 30, The New American Commentary (Nashville: Broadman & Holman Publishers, 1994), 405.

24. Joseph Thayers, Thayer's Greek-English Lexicon of the New Testament" http://www.studylight.org/lexicons/greek/gwview.cgi?n=2198. [Internet] (Accessed 26 July 2014).

25. Wayne Grudem, *Bible Doctrine: Essential Teachings of the Christian Faith* (Grand Rapids: Zondervan, 1999), 332.

26. Ray Steadman, "The Work and Blessing of the Spirit" http://ray-steadman.org/ephesians/richesinchrist.html [Internet] (Accessed 22 August 2014).

27. Jerry Vines, "The Tragedy of a Worldly Life" http://www.sermon-search.com/ sermon-outlines/10296/the-tragedy-of-a-worldly-life. [Internet] (Accessed 19 July 2014).

28. C. J. Mahaney, ed., *Worldliness: Resisting the Seduction of a Fallen World* (Wheaton: Crossway, 2008), 22.

29. Thomas A. Tarrants, III, "Hindrances to Discipleship: The World" http://www.cslewisinstitute.org/Hindrances_To_Discipleship_The_World_FullArticle. [Internet] (Accessed 21 August 2014).

30. Quoted by Steve Farrar, *Family Survival in the American Jungle* (Portland: Multnomah Press, 1991), 68.

31. Mahaney, *Worldliness*, 30-31.

32. Wikipedia, "Yusuf Ismail" http://en.wikipedia.org/wiki/Yusuf_İsmail. [Internet] (Accessed 27 July 2014).

33. Mahaney, Worldliness, 20.

34. Flora L. Williams, *The Shepherd's Guide through the Valley of Debt and Financial Change: A Comprehensive Manual for Financial Management, Counseling and Spiritual Guidance* (Bloomington, IN: AuthorHouse Digital Books: 2009), 199.

35. Ric Edelman, *The Truth about Money* (New York: Harper Collins, 2004), 298.

36. Randy Petersen, *Be Still, My Soul: The Inspiring Stories Behind 175 of the Most-Loved Hymns* (Carol Stream: Tyndale, 2014), 347.

37. Robert J. Morgan, *Then Sings My Soul* (Nashville: Thomas Nelson, 2003), 282-283.

38. Klyne Snodgrass, *Ephesians*, The NIV Application Commentary (Grand Rapids, MI: Zondervan, 1996), 339.

39. Norm Geisler, "Survey of Bible Doctrines" https://bible.org/book/export /html/6310. [Internet] (Accessed 8 July 2014).

40. C.S. Lewis, *The Screwtape Letters* (San Francisco: HarperOne, 2001), 58.

41. R. Kent Hughes, *Ephesians: The Mystery of the Body of Christ* (Wheaton: Crossway, 2013), 212.

42. Lewis, *Screwtape* Letters, 60-61.

43. Robert Cowley and Geoffrey Parker, *The Readers Companion to Military History* [1996] http://www.history.com/topics/world-war-ii/battle-of-the-bulge. [Internet] (Accessed 8 August 2014).

44. Russell D. Moore, "Why You're Tempted" http://www.christian-post.com/ news /why-youre-tempted-49803. [Internet] (Accessed 18 August 2014).

45. Prudence Labeach Pollard, *Raise a Leader God's Way* (Hagerstown, MD: Review and Herald Publishing, 2012), 17.

46. James H Ropes, *Epistle of James* (New York: Charles Scribner's Sons, 1916), 154.

47. Dietrich Bonhoeffer, *Creation and Fall – Temptation: Two Biblical Studies* (New York: Touchstone, 1997), 116-117.

48. Robby Gallaty, *Growing Up: How to Be a Disciple Who Makes Disciples* (Bloomington: CrossBooks, 2013), 120-121.

49. Stanford, *Green Letters*, 10-11.

50. Snodgrass, *Ephesians*, 354.

51. Charles Colson, *Who Speaks for God?* (Westchester, IL: Crossway Books, 1985), 68.

52. R. C. Sproul, *The Holiness of God* (Wheaton, IL: Tyndale, 1985), 67.

53. Ibid.

54. Ibid., 91–93.

55. Josephus, *Wars of the Jews*, VI. 1.8 as cited by Hughes, Ephesians, 232.

56. Charles R. Swindoll, *Job: a Man of Heroic Endurance* (Nashville: Thomas Nelson, 2004), 181.

57. Morgan, *Then Sings My Soul*, 14-15.

58. Howard Taylor, *Hudson Taylor's Spiritual Secret* (Chicago: Moody, 2009), 239.

59. E.M. Bounds, *Power Through Prayer* (Chicago, IL: Moody Publishers, 1979), 42.

60. David C Cook, *God's Little Devotional Journal for Women* (Tulsa: Honor Books, 2000), 180.

61. E.M. Bounds, *The E.M. Bounds Collection on Prayer* (Public Domain: 2002), 516.

62. Francis Wayland, *A Memoir of the Life and Labors of the Rev. Adoniram Judson*, (Boston: Phillips, Sampson, and Company, 1853), 459-461.

63. Markus Barth, *Ephesians, A New Translation with Introduction and Commentary* (New York, NY: Doubleday, 1974), 782.

64. Robert J. Morgan, *On This Day in Christian History* (Nashville: Thomas Nelson, 1997), 67.

65. Thomas R. Kelly, *A Testament of Devotion* (San Francisco: HarperOne, 1996), 10.

66. Brother Lawrence, *The Practice of the Presence of God* (New York, NY: Cosimo, Inc., 2006), 16.

Jesus said make disciples, not converts. **We can help.**

REPLICATE

REPLICATEMINISTRIES.ORG

DISCIPLESHIP BLUEPRINT

A Model for Making Disciples in the Local Church

Discipleship Blueprint is a weekend experience that allows you to spend time in the context of a local church actively engaging in discipleship. You'll have the opportunity to spend time with staff and walk alongside members as you:

- Learn how to plan, formulate, and develop a disciple-making culture in your church & its ministries (missions, women & men).

- Study Jesus' and other historical models for making disciples.

- Develop a comprehensive plan for raising up leaders in your church.

- Learn how to navigate issues that arise in your D-Groups.

- Participate in a D-Group led by an experienced disciple-maker.

- Consider principles and strategies for starting D-Groups & multiplying mature believers in your own context when you return.

REPLICATEMINISTRIES.ORG/BLUEPRINT